SWAT TEAM DEVELOPMENT AND DEPLOYMENT

By Michael Holm

Assistant Special Agent in Charge (Retired)
Drug Enforcement Administration

VARRO

P R E S S

SWAT Team Development and Deployment

Michael Holm

VARRO PRESS
P.O. Box 8413
Shawnee Mission, Kansas 66208 USA
Tel: 913-385-2034 ~ Fax: 913-385-2039
Web: www.varropress.com

Publisher's Cataloging-in-Publication
(Provided by Quality Books, Inc.)

Holm, Michael, 1946-
    SWAT team developmment and deployment / by Michael
Holm. -- 1st ed.
    p. cm.
    LCCN 00-134767
    ISBN 1-88864-466-4

    1. Police--Special weapons and tactics units.
    2. Police training. 3. Police--Equipment and Supplies
    I. Title

HV8080.S64H65 2002   363.2'32
                QBI00-901517

Printed and bound in the United States of America

SWAT TEAM DEVELOPMENT AND DEPLOYMENT

TABLE OF CONTENTS

DEDICATION

GUSTAVE H. HOLM

To you who answered the call of your country and served in its Armed Forces to bring about the total defeat of the enemy, I extend the heartfelt thanks of a grateful Nation. As one of the Nation's finest, you undertook the most severe task one can be called upon to perform. Because you demonstrated the fortitude, resourcefulness and calm judgment necessary to carry out that task, we now look to you for leadership and example in further exalting our country in peace.

THE WHITE HOUSE

Harry S. Truman

FOREWORD

Special Weapons and Tactics is a topic that is complex and multi-faceted. Mike Holm's text covers a very broad range of issues, and is an easy read for the law enforcement officer who is looking for solid concise information that is easily located and absorbed. The author has a long history of practical experience in law enforcement and in special weapons' assignments.

Mike Holm has an enthusiasm for SWAT and his emotional attachment to law enforcement is evident throughout the book. He expresses himself with a bit of humor and a lot of heart. Throughout his career with the Drug Enforcement Administration, Mike gathered numerous friends and admirers from all areas of law enforcement. No cop who asked for assistance from Mike was turned away. With this book, he continues to help. All of the basics in the categories that are addressed in each chapter are clearly identified and thoughtfully presented. Chapter 8 on the construction of a shooting house is typical of Mike and his book. He covers all of the practical issues including arguments in favor of a shooting house and all of the areas of resistance a team might expect when contemplating this essential training asset.

I am honored to offer this foreword on behalf of a truly professional veteran of law enforcement. His book is like his career, honest, to the point, and a valuable asset that will remain relevant for many years to come.

—Ron McCarthy, LAPD Retired

PREFACE

I wrote this book because there is a need for operators to pass their experience to the next generation. There is a definite hunger for more tactical knowledge in the tactical community, and there have been numerous requests for a "tactical manual", but this is countered by agencies' reluctance to document and distribute their tactics. It is logical to protect your tactics from falling into the hands of the adversary. An agency also must protect itself from civil litigation and faces a high probability that a manual or regulations would be discoverable and could be used against them in court. With this in mind, I structured this book to cover the basics and not compromise any classified operational tactics.

I would be remiss in not pointing out that almost everything I know about this subject was passed on to me by the true icons in this field who were gracious, patient, and always supportive. They are my heroes.

We fight evil and death. We restore order. We are committed to a higher calling. There are situations when we find ourselves at times and places where the mission and destiny are more important than safety. I hope this book will help you prepare for those moments and wish you Godspeed.

—Michael Holm

INTRODUCTION

This book is structured as a guide to select personnel, equip and train them to conduct high-risk operations. Mission specific equipment and tactics are discussed and actual operations are cited as examples. The conclusion discusses ramifications of operations and an overview of the future for SWAT and SPECOPS.

CHAPTER 1

Historical Background

The origins of specialized teams in the United States can be traced back to the beginning of U. S. military history. The necessity for sharpshooters, commandos, and rangers was recognized as early as the Revolutionary War. Army Rangers, Airborne units, and Special Forces led to the development of "Blue Light" - the first U. S. counter-terrorist unit and predecessor to DELTA. The U. S. Navy established Underwater Demolition Teams (UDT) which were the predecessor of the SEALs (Sea Air and Land). From the SEALs, the counter-terrorist unit SEAL Team-6 was formed under Navy Special War Command (NAVSPECWARCOM). SEAL Team-6 expanded to a large well equipped Development Group (DEVGRP). The U. S. Marines have special units called Force Recon. All three U. S. military services have developed tactics and training for fighting on urban terrain, and have constructed MOUT sites (Military Operations on Urban Terrain) with shooting houses for live fire training.

Other pioneers of counter terrorist and SWAT tactics are recognized for their leadership in this arena. The Israelis have

Sayeret units in each army zone command. These units specialize in counter terrorist action and hostage rescue. The most famous operation was operation "Thunderbolt" - the hostage rescue at Entebbe, Uganda in 1976 conducted by Sayeret Matkal. The Federal Republic of Germany established the venerable GSG-9 - famous for the rescue of hostages from a hijacked Lufthansa airliner in Mogadishu, Somalia in 1977. The United Kingdom established the Special Air Service (SAS) which has seen extensive service in Asia, South East Asia, Africa, the Middle East (including Desert Storm), the Falklands War, and Northern Ireland. The SAS "Pagoda Team" is famous for operation "Nimrod" - the rescue of hostages in the Iranian Embassy at Princes Gate, London, England in 1980. The French established GIGN who left their calling card in 1994 rescuing hostages from a hijacked Air France airliner that had flown from Algeria to Marseille, France. The four well-armed, fanatic, terrorists were killed.

The FBI developed SWAT Teams to support requests, not only from their agency, but other law enforcement agencies as well. In the early 1980's, the FBI established the Hostage Rescue Team (HRT) based at Quantico, Virginia.

In the mid 1980's, a team of terrorists flew from Lebanon to Cyprus, and then to Italy. They boarded a cruise ship called the "Achille Lauro". During the highjacking, they killed an American citizen. The ship anchored in the Alexandria, Egypt harbor. Egyptian authorities negotiated the safe release of the hostages and safe passage for the terrorists by air out of the country. NAVSPECWARCOM was monitoring these activities, and the aircraft transporting the terrorists was diverted by F-14 Tomcats to Siganella, Italy which happens to host a U. S. Navy Base. The plane was surrounded by SEALs and a stalemate ensued. The Italian authorities refused to authorize an assault on the aircraft. The terrorists were allowed to depart Italy.

HRT subsequently lured a member of the organization (PLF) onto a yacht off the coast of Cyprus to negotiate a narcotic transaction. He was arrested, transported to the United States, and tried for the highjacking of the ship and murder of the U. S. citizen. This is officially known as: "extraterritorial rendition".

The Secret Service established a Counter Assault Team (CAT) for Presidential protection. They are well-trained, well-armed, and very well equipped. CAT has the most sophisticated electronic counter measures of any protective service in the world.

Law enforcement organizations in the United States are well structured and paramilitary. Many policies and procedures are patterned after the military and tailored to suit the civilian atmosphere. In the 1960's, a number of law enforcement related incidents occurred that caused law enforcement management to re-evaluate their capability to respond to certain crises.

On August 1, 1966 Charles Whitman, a former U. S. Marine marksman, entered the Administration Building of the University of Texas Austin with an assortment of rifles and other weaponry. Before he was killed by two police officers, he had killed 15 people (one unborn baby) and wounded 31 from as far away as two blocks. This became known as the "Texas Tower Incident".

Both Los Angeles Police Department (LAPD) and LA Sheriff's Department (LASD) encountered incidents that involved barricaded, well-armed, suspects such as the Symbionese Liberation Army, Black Panthers, and hard core felons including suspects who had killed police officers. LAPD formed a SWAT Team by adding a 60 man platoon (D Platoon) to their Metropolitan Unit. LASD established a platoon called Special Enforcement Bureau (SEB). These were the first fully dedicated SWAT Teams in the United States, and they quickly sought training from the military. One event that greatly enhanced their development was the preparation and interagency coordination for the 1984 Olympics in Los Angeles. Their equipment, sophisticated tactics, and relationship with U. S. law enforcement, intelligence, and counter-terrorist units remains superb to this day.

Most major metropolitan communities have a response capability patterned after LAPD SWAT and/or LASD/SEB. Some are not fully dedicated, some are decentralized, and some are regional teams with representation from departments in the area. Most federal agencies have decentralized teams.

CHAPTER 2

Team Structure

The classical assault team was based on the military "fire team".

TEAM LEADER (LDR)

On police departments the Team Leader is usually a Sergeant. He is a member of the entry team and controls it's movement and tactical execution of the mission. He is experienced, tactically proficient, and familiar with all positions on the team. He conducts the operational briefing and ensures members are properly equipped. He controls communications and provides situation reports (SITREPS) to the commander. He controls team movement through a structure and ensures all danger areas are cleared. Because he is the ranking officer in the danger area, he has the authority to abort, assault, and extract in a compromise or hostile contact situation. After the structure has been cleared, he notifies perimeter security that the team is exiting the structure.

POINT MAN/SCOUT (PM/S)

The Point Man (PM) or Scout(S) is the number one position in the assault team line up. He reconnoiters the location and suggests entry points and team positions. He determines direction of entry, leads the team, and provides protection from a surprise assault. The Point Man controls the pace of the team's movement. He is armed with a submachine gun SMG or shotgun always pointed at danger areas which includes the point of entry during initial approach.

BACK UP MAN (BUM)

The Back Up Man is an assistant to the Point Man and follows him into all areas to be cleared and covers the direction that the Point Man does not cover. If the PM clears right, the BUM clears left. This procedure eliminates the need to "predetermine" which direction they will clear when entering an area to be cleared. He is armed with a SMG or shotgun.

OMNI MAN/GAS MAN/GRENADIER(OMNI/GS/GRD)

This member is responsible for special equipment necessary for the operation and the delivery of chemical agents. Equipment could include rope, rapelling equipment, hooks, lights, noise flash devices, less lethal munitions, and breaching equipment. He provides security for the team. Some teams have back-ups for this position. They are armed with SMGs or shotguns.

REAR SECURITY (RS)

RS is a counter sniper and protects the team from attack from the rear. The RS is armed with a rifle with semi-automatic capability. Iron sights, or scopes and optics that allow instant target acquisition are preferred. The RS usually only enters the structure upon the LDR's call. This prevents hostiles from maneuvering around and behind the team.

SNIPER/MARKSMAN(S)

The Sniper provides long rifle support for the team and is many times in a position to take the first shot to protect the team or neutralize the suspect. He is also in a position to pass real time intelligence to the Commander and Leader regarding the suspect's activities.

OBSERVER/SPOTTER (O)

The Observer assists the Sniper and provides security. He is also a sniper and can relieve the primary sniper. The Sniper and Observer deploy and function as a team.

COMMANDER (C)

Police Departments' SWAT Commanders are usually Lieutenants. This provides liaison for the team with superiors in the chain of command and absorbs pressure that would otherwise be borne by the Team Leader who needs to concentrate on tactics. SWAT Team Commanders should be hand picked, selected for their integrity, work history, and past performance. They should be physically fit and meet all criteria and qualifications for the SWAT Team. They should know tactics and weapons and train with their fellow officers. It is recommended that they have previous SWAT experience. If not, they should be given one year to meet the criteria. A SWAT Commander must consistently make intelligent decisions under pressure.

TEMS/PARAMEDICS(MD)

Paramedics are sworn Peace Officers cross-trained in tactics. They are prepared to handle medical emergencies involving team members, civilians, and suspects. There are doctors who are members of SWAT Teams in a Tactical Emergency Medical Support (TEMS) program. Paramedics and TEMS doctors perform their duties unarmed because of the possibility that a panicked or disoriented patient may attempt to grab their weapon while being treated.

SWAT TEAM CONFIGURATION

SWAT Teams are activated pursuant to criteria and based on the team's configuration.

CENTRALIZED-FULL TIME

Centralized Teams have the least difficulty activating team members. Usually half the platoon is in training status, and the other half is on stand-by or assigned to patrolling high crime rate areas, stake outs, dignitary security, or security for planned events. They are notified of an incident by radio and proceed to a rally point or station. Sometimes a second team is activated in case there is another "Call Out".

DECENTRALIZED TEAMS

Few departments are able to staff full time SWAT Teams. An activation procedure is initiated usually by pager for call outs. Members are required to be on stand-by to ensure that there is sufficient manpower to meet the crisis.

Regional Teams have been established where a number of law enforcement agencies contribute manpower and logistics to meet the needs of the municipalities involved. This concept requires the most coordination and standardization. The main difficulty encountered in De-Centralized and Regional Teams is the lack of training and resultant degradation of capability.

CRITERIA FOR REQUESTING A SWAT TEAM

This policy must be established before activation occurs. Not only should the entire department be fully aware of the activation policy, but adjoining jurisdictions and prosecutors as well. When developing criteria, existing policy should be considered as well as legal precedent. It is generally held that, because of the force that a SWAT Team possesses, they should not generally be used for misdemeanor arrests.

Deployment is based upon the commission or suspicion of an inherently dangerous felony such as:

- Armed, barricaded felony suspect
- Armed, barricaded suspect/hostage situation
- Sniper
- Preventive deployment to provide dignitary security
- Deployment to high crime rate area
- Felony high risk warrant service
    - Criminal history for violence
    - Violent crime committed
    - Weapons have been used in the commission of a crime and would probably be used again against police
    - Heavy fortification - bars on windows and doors
    - Armed sentries

CHAPTER 3

Selection of Personnel

In earlier SWAT team development, there was an overemphasis on marksmanship. Although marksmanship is a critical element, it is not the exclusive or predominant factor. It is preferable to have department certified firearms instructors on the team, but they must meet all of the other standards. Past SWAT and military experience is also beneficial, but it is re-iterated that SWAT operators with no previous experience have developed into excellent team members. It is recommended that police departments require two years of patrol experience to enhance coordination and communication with the department they support. For example, a SWAT operator needs to be familiar with department radio procedures and have an understanding of department protocol in a crisis situation. Patrol experience also seasons the officer to develop a "command presence" when arresting uncooperative suspects. I have seen officers with military combat experience hands' shake during their first felony arrest. Police work is a specialized field and SWAT is a very specialized and stressful arena that requires a seasoned operator.

There are written psychological tests that can be administered as well as clinical psychologists on contract with most departments to assist in screening. The Commander and Team Leader are encouraged to participate in all screening and interview phases. Quite frankly, the fate of the team is greatly impacted by the selection process.

SWAT is very athletic. The rigors of deployment demand the highest level of physical fitness or the safety and effectiveness of the team is negatively impacted. Also, remember law enforcement officers are civil servants, and the citizens expect them to win. Appearances can be deceptive, and it is probably the most subjective part of the selection process. An applicant might appear not to be physically fit, or by his appearance, it might be obvious he is not physically fit. Either way, the applicant should be advised of this and given the opportunity to correct the situation and re-apply.

The applicant interview can provide a great deal of insight into the character and motivation of the applicant. Some teams require a written application and autobiography to determine written communication skills, also an oral briefing is also required. A photograph of the applicant is required. It is recommended that the Commander, Team Leader, and clinical psychologist (if deemed necessary) participate in the interview. Questions should be determined in advance and conducted in an organized, expeditious manner. The applicant should be thoroughly briefed as to the nature of the team mission and what is expected. It is important to determine how the applicant relates to the team concept. One of the problems encountered in the psychological screening phase is to what action the department is required to take if the applicant demonstrates a significant problem that had previously been undetected. It should be determined in advance how these situations should be handled.

Age, in and of itself, should not be a factor provided the standards can be met; however, with possible exception of the Commander and Team Leader, it might be advisable to establish a maximum age for entry applicants.

Many tests have been devised to assess physical condition and agility. The trend is to make them more job related. This is probably the result of administrative and legal appeals by unsuccessful candidates. Some of the earlier challenges were successful when the department was questioned as to how many times an officer was required to do push-ups and sit-ups in the performance of his duty.

LASD/SEB developed a job-related proficiency test for applicants. This test was reviewed by the Kinesiology Department of the University of California at Los Angeles. Because of the success of this test, the following description is included:

The applicant must wear a SWAT Team uniform, boots, protective vest, and web pistol belt with sidearm when taking this test. The test begins with a 100-yard run to the first station:

Station 1: Six Foot Wall Climb - simulates what might be required during a "call out"

Station 2: Underground Culvert - crawl through ten foot underground pipe simulating checking for suspect

Station 3: Monkey Bar Traverse - 20 foot length of monkey bars to test upper body strength and coordination

Station 4: Open Window and Crawl Space - applicant negotiates a 30-by-30 inch window four feet off the ground to duplicate entry into a structure

Station 5: Body Transport - a live "victim" weighing 165 pounds must be dragged 15 feet simulating moving a wounded team member to a point of safety

Station 6: Five-foot Wall Climb - duplicates Station 1 with a wall of less height

Station 7: Chain Link Fence Climb - scale eight foot fence duplicating action taken during SWAT activities

Station 8: Quarter-mile Run - measures applicant's ability to respond quickly to situations over concrete and grass surfaces

At the conclusion of the run, applicants continue through Stations 1 through 7 a second time without stopping. This concludes the timed portion of the test. After a 15-20 minute rest period, the second phase is conducted with no time limits:

Station 1: Thirty-five foot Ladder Climb - simulates building ascent

Station 2: Thirty-five foot Rappel - simulates free rappel from a helicopter

Station 3: Twenty-foot Rope Ascent - tests upper body strength for climbing structures

Station 4: Ladder Descent - tests agility in descending from a building roof by means of a stationary ladder

Station 5: Parallel Bar Traverse - applicant must traverse a 10-foot long set of parallel bars from one end to the other and back - this tests arm strength

This test has proven to be a very valid way of objectively evaluating an applicant's ability to perform SWAT related physical tasks. An unsuccessful applicant may be allowed to take the test again after a predetermined period of time. SWAT Team members should be required to pass this test on a quarterly basis.

The LAPD SWAT Platoon (D Platoon) tests only when there are vacancies. Applicants must already be members of the Metropolitan Division. The first phase is the oral interview. All applicants were asked the same questions. Evaluators were asked to look for dedication, decisiveness, initiative, and of great importance, the ability to understand training. Applicants were issued blue running shorts, boots, and a white T-shirt bearing an assigned letter/number combination. They were separated into five-man teams, each with a designated (but rotating) team leader. Evaluators were given cards to take notes. The test consisted of two days at city facilities and three days at a Marine Base. The general areas tested included: physical fitness, firearms proficiency, rappelling, and the ability to function as a member of a team. At the end of the testing, evaluators were gathered to discuss their ratings and the notations on their cards.

This concept could easily be adopted by another agency. Those applicants who successfully passed were assigned to a six-week SWAT Training Course and were on probation for one year. Some teams assign probationary officers to perimeter security. They are assigned to an entry team after completion of the probationary period.

Screening processes are usually challenged by unsuccessful candidates administratively, in a State Superior Court, or in Federal Court usually under Title VII of the Civil Rights Act of 1964. Physical ability tests must be job related and not based on stereotypes of what the job entails. Court decisions have held that law enforcement agencies have considerable latitude to develop and enforce reasonable health and fitness standards for law enforcement employment. There are many validated fitness tests for SWAT Team applicant screening that can be used as a guide to develop a program.

A complete background investigation should be conducted after all other phases are completed because it can be the most time consuming. A checklist is often helpful to ensure all pertinent data is gathered. The applicant's unit commander, immediate supervisor, and his peers should be interviewed. Questions should include those relating to the applicant's background, outside interests, experience, performance, team work, and ability to get along with people. Marital status and stability should also tactfully be explored, and an interview of the spouse can shed light on their support. Considerable weight should be given to the supervisor and unit commander's recommendations. The applicant's personnel file and financial record should be reviewed. The applicant should be given the opportunity to respond to any derogatory information and answer any questions the background investigator might have.

The decision for acceptability should be made by the Commander with input from the Team Leader and members of the team. It is the responsibility of the Commander to ensure that chroniism and discrimination are not allowed. Large departments usually have the luxury of having more qualified applicants than vacancies. However, this might not be the case in smaller organizations. New teams and developing teams might not have the interest that an established, successful, and prestigious team enjoys. Rather than lower the standards, it is recommended that vacancies be re-advertised and candidates be spotted and recruited. There are some supervisors and unit commanders who do not support the SWAT concept, and they will dissuade their officers and even block their candidacy, especially if the applicant is one of their top performers. These same individuals will also disrupt training for de-centralized teams by "finding" something else for the officer to do when training is scheduled. This type of person is called a "Marplot". A Marplot is an individual whose sole mission in life is to disrupt someone else's program. Every agency has them. They tend to gravitate towards staff positions in headquarters. A Commander will be required to constantly deal with Marplots. The best strategy is to go over their heads. Marplots fear power. They remind me of how Winston Churchill described Nazi Germany: "They are at your throat, or they are at your feet."

CHAPTER 4

Communications, Equipment, and Weapons Selection

COMMUNICATIONS

Secure communications for each team member to include the assault team and perimeter security is essential to avoid compromise and provide command and control. There are three basic configurations: (1) throat microphone with ear piece, (2) "whisper" microphone on headset with audio attachment that vibrates into cheekbone, and (3) ballistic helmet equipped with noise dampening earphones for ear protection and "whisper" microphone. The ballistic helmet is preferred, because most other ear protection will not fit under a ballistic helmet. Fifty percent of the officers killed wearing body armor were shot in the head. Ballistic helmets are essential. Ear protection with noise dampening capability reduces the sound of gunfire and noise flash devices but allows, or even amplifies, ambient noise to be received. Snipers will probably prefer not to wear the ballistic helmet, but need secure communications as well. The Tactical Operations Center and Command Post will need the basic base radio configuration, and a repeater is also recommended. Cellular telephones are recommended for all supervisory and command personnel. Please remember they are not secure.

EQUIPMENT

Uniforms should fit the environment they are used in. A gray camouflage might be best suited for urban deployments. Black, olive drab, and navy blue are also popular. In rural areas woodland pattern camouflage fatigues are preferred. Desert fatigues are suited for arid areas. During "Desert Storm", some reconnaissance teams wore desert fatigue pants and woodland pattern jackets, because the flat terrain silhouetted them against the sky at night. Remember the key to concealment is silhouette, shape, and shine. The most important factor is that the uniform must be identifiable as a police uniform. Nomex material is recommended, to include the balaklava hood, especially in helicopter and drug laboratory operations.

Head cover should be selected in accordance with the tactical situation. Knitted wool caps are useful in certain situations. Baseball caps are only suitable for training and should be uniform. The bill prevents the operator from seeing up in tactical situations.

Undershirts should be consistent with the uniform and should only bear the unit or department logo. Socks should be consistent with the uniform. Boots should be light weight and support the ankle. They should be dark in color. Weather and terrain factors might necessitate the purchase of more than one type of footwear.

Nomex military aviation gloves, rapelling gloves, and heavier winter gloves are essential. Watches should not beep. Speaking of beeps; put your pager on vibrate or secure it.

A low rise SAS type holster with thumb-operated restraining strap that accommodates a light mounted on a pistol is recommended. This allows the operator to access the pistol from any position. Leg mounted noise flash device pouches are recommended.

Body armor should be level 3A and allow the operator to shoulder a long weapon, prone out, crouch, climb, run, and twist. Ceramic inserts should be included as an accessory. The body armor manufacturer can build pouches into the vest to suit your needs or a separate load bearing vest can be purchased. Gas masks should have a full window as opposed to separate eye lenses. A filter that can be moved from right to left is essential to facilitate shouldering a weapon.

A quality knife is essential, but it is not intended as a weapon for SWAT. Goggles are one of the most important pieces of equipment. They should be shatterproof and not fog. A wooly pully type sweater is recommended. Elbow and knee pads are essential protective equipment. Rappelling equipment, flashlight, handcuffs, and flexcuffs are necessary. When training with other teams, and through your own experience, you will be exposed to equipment that will enhance your team's capability. Your inventory will expand over time as a result of experience.

NECESSARY SWAT PERSONAL EQUIPMENT

The following is a suggested list of SWAT Team personal equipment and approximate costs. It is not a product endorsement:

BDU Jacket $100
Boots 100
Utilities (2) pair 150
Nomex Gloves 50
Nomex Balaklava Hood 30
Belt 15

Rappel Gloves 30
Rappel Equipment 100
Equipment Bag 100
Holster 50
Noise Flash Device Pouch 50
Gas Mask 260
Gas Mask Leg Carrier 150
Ballistic Helmet
     w/ear protection and radio accessories . . . 2,000
Elbow and Knee Pads 40
Radio 2,000
Goggles 30
Ballistic Level 3 Vest 300-1,500
Light for SMG 100
Light for Shotgun 100
Light for Pistol 80

Total $5,835 - $7,035

A great deal of research is required when purchasing equipment, especially the "big ticket" items that you will be required to function with for some time to come. It is highly recommended that established SWAT Teams be consulted. Vendor demonstrations are also helpful.

WEAPONS SELECTION

Firearms, as we know them, have developed to about as close to their maximum potential as they can get. Bolt action rifles and semi-automatic pistols have been on the scene since the turn of the century. Both the .45 caliber and 9mm parabellum pistol have been in existence for over eighty years.

World War II brought on the advent of the light machine gun, submachine gun, and assault rifle. Germany developed the prototype for the M-60 that is currently in U. S. inventory. The

Russians copied the German assault rifle concept, and the AK-47 was designed. Assault rifles like the FN/FAL and Israeli Galil were developed. The Israelis also developed the Uzi, the Italians the Berretta, and the Germans the H & K 9mm submachine guns.

The Vietnam Was era saw the emergence of the M-60, M-16, M-203, M-49 grenade launcher and Light Anti Tank Weapon (LAW). The North Vietnamese and Viet Cong used the AK-47, Dushka .52 caliber machine gun, rocket propelled grenade (RPG), and RPD light machine gun all produced by Russia or China. The above weapons played a major role in the development of small unit tactics that have become part of the military doctrine that has influenced SWAT tactics in law enforcement agencies.

In addition to law enforcement and military development, big game hunters influenced the development of hunting rifles and a great deal of experimentation with ballistics occurred. Many calibers have been developed with many types, shapes, and weights of bullets. Parallels can sometimes be made on the effects of bullets on big game and humans. Both have skin, cartiledge, bone, muscle, soft tissue, hair, water, and body cavities. All disciplines have developed scopes, night vision equipment, and range finders.

With all of this research having been conducted, the tactical community has made some general consensus. The .308 caliber bolt action rifle is the primary weapon of choice for police snipers. The semi-automatic .308 and .223 are also chosen for their sniper/counter sniper capability.

The 9mm submachine gun is the weapon of choice for most law enforcement and counter-terrorist units. The 9mm pistol followed by the .45 caliber pistol is the sidearm of choice.

Semi-automatic 12 gauge shotguns are preferred over pump action shotguns because of increased firepower. Large capacity magazines are preferred in both.

Grenade launchers that are 37 mm are preferred for the deployment of CS, OC (oleoresin capsicum derived from cayenne pepper) and less lethal munitions.

The M-60 light machine gun is the light machine gun of choice. DEA also uses the .223 caliber Squad Automatic Weapon (SAW) in South America along with the M-60 and M-16. This is an example of how military training from the U. S. Army Rangers, Special Forces, and Navy SEALs influences a civilian law enforcement agency's tactics and weapons selection. DEA chose the Colt 9mm SMG because it is compatible in function with the M-16A2.

One of the best ways to enhance the performance of your weapons system is to choose the best bullets available. Most ammunition is rated higher than it will actually perform by the manufacturer. Furthermore, ballistic gelatin tests are really only good for comparison of how bullets differ in their performance in that medium. Many departments issue ammunition that does not perform adequately in shootings.

The key to wound efficiency is diameter, weight, and velocity. A high velocity, thin skinned, rapidly expanding bullet is preferred. A non-expanding bullet leaves a wound that is only the diameter of the bullet. A high velocity, quick expanding bullet hitting the heart-lung area will expand when entering and spray pieces of jacket and chunks of core throughout a cavity causing maximum incapacitation. The bullet with less expansion will not destroy as much vital tissue; consequently, it does not kill as fast. In order to drive an expanded bullet with it's large frontal area through bone and muscle and vital organs, a large portion of the bullet must remain intact to furnish the mass for the momentum required for penetration. To retain sectional density, a very strong jacket is needed to allow penetration. The jacket should be thin at the front, and the core should be soft enough to flow outward expanding the jacket as it penetrates. The jacket must gradually become thicker to stop expansion around the middle of the bullet. The jacket should be ductile enough so it does not break as it peals back but forms a large frontal area that destroys tissue as it penetrates. Comparisons should be made as to what the bullet weighs after penetration to the original weight. Too much disintegration will reduce effectiveness. Also, a 9mm bullet fired from an SMG will travel 200 FPS faster than from a pistol. You might obtain desired expansion from the SMG, but little expansion from your pistol. This will require different ammunition for your pistol or the selection of a heavier caliber.

WEAPONS PRICES

The basic prices for weapons are as follows:

.308 caliber bolt action rifle, accurized,
  bull barrel, w/scope $2,000

.308 caliber accurized semi-automatic
  rifle w/scope 1,800

.223 caliber semi-automatic rifle w/scope 1,400

9mm SMG (Colt 500 or HK MP-5) 1,200

12 gauge semi-automatic shotgun 800

12 gauge pump shotgun 250

9mm pistol 500

HK .45 caliber "USSOCOM" pistol 750

M-60 Light Machine Gun 1,800-2,500

.223 caliber Squad Automatic Weapon (SAW) ... 1,200

37 mm grenade launcher system 500

CHAPTER 5

Vehicle Equipment and Team Driving Techniques

One of the most important phases of an operation, and one that is most often overlooked, is transportation to the objective. Departments use either marked or unmarked cars. Unmarked cars should be equipped with emergency lights and sirens. The Team Leader and at least one additional vehicle should have a public address system. The Team Leader and at least one member should have a cellular telephone that can be removed from the vehicle for communications. (The reader will see the "redundancy" theory throughout this book.) For those vehicles that are taken to the operator's residence, equipment security is essential. This can be accomplished by alarming the vehicle, and installing a manual cut-off switch as well to prevent auto theft. Weapons can be secured by locked storage racks that are electronically activated for quick access. Also racks that are bolted down and padlocked can be used. A locked "raid box" can be bolted down in the trunk to store weapons, radios, ammunition, and pyrotechnics. A chain and padlock to further secure the trunk can easily and cheaply enhance equipment security. A steel plate installed to protect the trunk lock will also protect equipment stored in the trunk.

Different types of vehicles can enhance a team's operational effectiveness. Armored vehicles can be acquired or loaned out from the Department of Defense and Department of Energy. Armored car companies also often donate their surplus vehicles to law enforcement agencies. Vehicles seized from drug traffickers can be forfeited and put into service. Vans and utility vehicles can be used to transport team members and equipment. It is recommended that the team be transported in more than one vehicle. (Redundancy) A removable sky light installed over the back (second seat) of a utility vehicle is excellent for deploying counter snipers to protect the team approaching the crisis area. LAPD/SWAT devised a hydraulically operated platform installed on the bed of a truck for second story entrances. (Known as: "SWAT In The Box").

The following team driving techniques were described in *A Guide to The Development of Special Weapons and Tactics Teams* by John A. Kolman, (1982) Springfield, IL, Charles Thomas, Publisher.

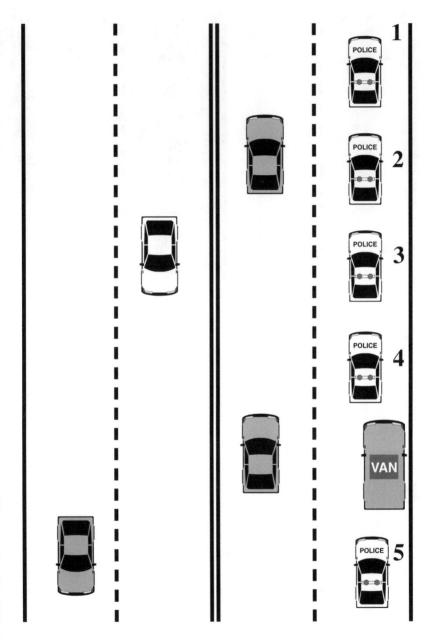

Swat Team Proceeding in Convoy - Note Van Offset to Allow Last Vehicle Vision to the Front

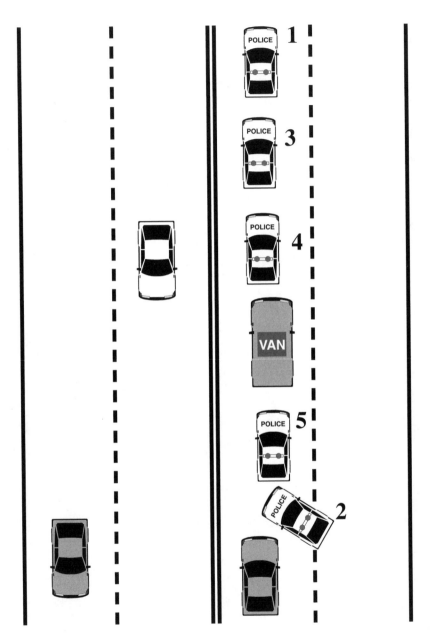

Vehicle Number Two Blocks Traffic In Number One Lane, Other Convoy Vehicles Pass In Front Of Him

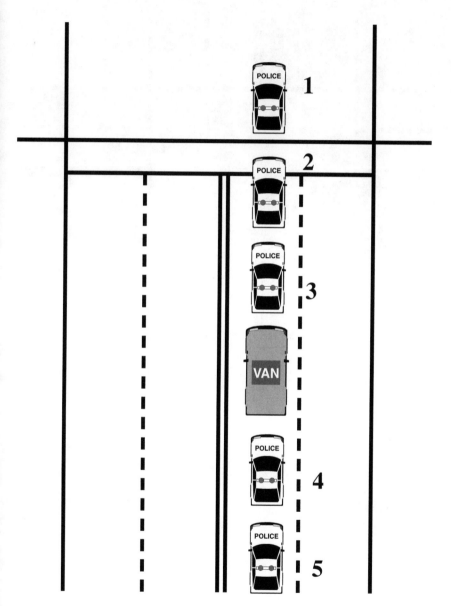

Convoy Enters Intersection Slowly With Emergency Lights And Sirens

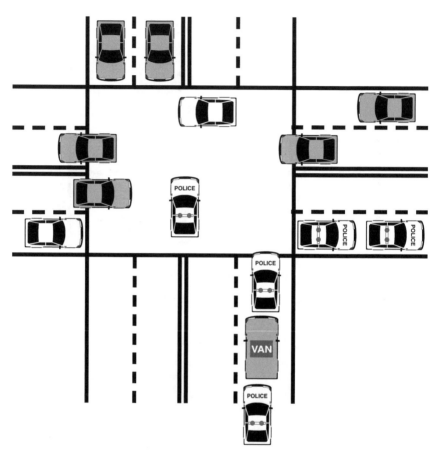

One Vehicle Blocks Traffic While Convoy Turns Right

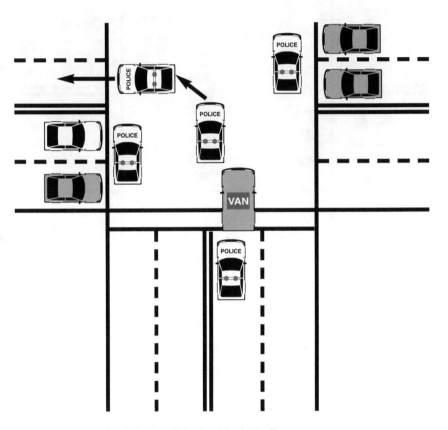

Convoy Turns Left While Two Vehicles Block Traffic

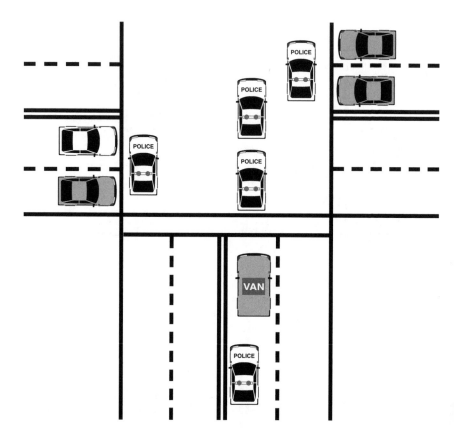

Two Vehicles Block Traffic To Allow Convoy To Proceed

CHAPTER 6

Movement Under Fire/ Immediate Action Drills

When an operator comes under hostile fire, he must be able to react appropriately. Prior planning may prevent encountering hostile fire. But, if hostile fire is encountered, the operator must take action immediately. The action taken will be the result of previous training.

The first principal is to always move as if you are under constant hostile observation. Remain tactical at all times. Reconnaissance, target observation, identifying key positions for assault team and snipers, and the use of cover and concealment are principles to be observed. Cover protects you from weapons fire. Exterior cover could be a brick or cement wall, fire hydrant, cement curb, ditch, or mound of dirt sufficient to stop a bullet (approximately three feet will stop .223 and .308). Interior cover is usually less available. Most buildings have wood frames and plasterboard walls that will not stop small arms fire. Keep this in mind when engaging an aggressor inside a structure. Many times firing through walls can be effective. Ricochets have a tendency to hug the ground and walls by about six inches.

Concealment protects the operator from observation. It may or may not be cover. Examples of exterior concealment would be brush, trees, fences, and tall grass. Interior concealment would be walls and partitions. Remember, most interior concealment is not cover.

Maintain sound and light discipline, be prepared for hostile fire, and to react immediately by building up fire superiority. Take the "high ground". Time and coordinate advance by easily identifiable features. Continuous, rapid, aggressive movement has proven to lessen your chances of being a casualty. Close on the enemy to take him by surprise, put him on the defensive, and allow more accurate and effective fire. This will help convince the enemy that you are a superior force and demoralize him. The rule of thumb when assaulting over open terrain is to move rapidly saying to yourself: "I'm up. He sees me. I'm down." When you prone out, roll left or right, because shooters tend to track their targets.

The low profile is the instinctive reaction under fire. The low crawl sacrifices speed for concealment. The high crawl sacrifices concealment for speed. There is a high fatigue factor in both. For advancing over open terrain, use alternate suppressive fire in lieu of cover. Be prepared for hostile fire, and to react immediately building up fire superiority. Rapid, aggressive movement while remaining low is best when hostile fire is encountered. At short distances, a shotgun is effective; over ten yards, cover fire should be by submachine gun or rifle. Cover fire often necessitates firing over or near a team member. This cannot be done with a shotgun. Shotguns are not recommended for hostage rescue operations. Handguns are defensive weapons and should only be brought into action when long guns malfunction or exhaust their ammunition supply. There are few exceptions to this axiom.

Movement under fire is psychologically stressful, but not more stressful than movement under the anticipation of fire. Movement has to be planned as completely yet, as rapidly, as possible in almost all cases. To achieve success, coordination is the key factor. All movement under fire, or, anticipated fire is to be done so that the individual or team moving is covered by friendly fire, or the immediate capability of friendly fire. The choices of weapons can enhance or detract from success of the mission. However, too many, or too much weaponry can hamper movement; and, will detract from, or cause the failure of a mission. The above principals can help assure success.

It is recommended that SWAT Teams study the tactics of other teams and adopt the best ideas and practices that fit their agency. Most SWAT Team Leaders have "compromise authority" to abort or assault if team security is compromised while approaching the objective. "Action on hostile contact" immediate action drills should be developed. It should be pre-determined what action should be taken if an ambush or sniper is encountered.

The term ambush derives from the French word "ambusier" which means "attack from the forest". A SWAT operator should know the basic types of ambushes and be trained to react with self-sufficiency, resourcefulness, ingenuity, common knowledge, and aggression. The purpose of an ambush is to inflict casualties, destroy equipment, and harass. A small group can successfully engage a superior force. The elements of an ambush are: surprise, violence, superiority and coordination of fire, choice of terrain and site, and control of fire.

In a "Line" ambush, the aggressors are lined-up along an expected avenue of approach. When the main body of the approaching force gets into the "kill zone", the aggressors deliver a high volume of fire, and/or explosives on the force.

The "L Shaped" ambush is the same as the Line Ambush, except that there is an aggressor force at either the head or end of the approaching force, which shoots down into the force from either the front or rear.

In a "V Shaped" ambush fire is directed down from both sides of the kill zone. Firing from high positions downward reduces the possibility of crossfire. Snipers can be used very effectively in this configuration.

In an "Area" ambush, the hostiles wait for the force to enter a specific area and then deliver devastating fire. The same basic formations can be used for "Vehicle" ambushes. Individuals in vehicles are confined in the vehicle and their movements are limited. The only hope for surviving a vehicle ambush is to drive through, or out, of the ambush site or exit the vehicle and fight your way to safety.

Ambushes are sometimes used to channel forces into a secondary ambush. The variety of ambushes is only limited by an individual's imagination. The famous Chinese General Sun Tsu wrote about how to react in tactical situations. One situation was referred to as "death ground". He wrote: "When on death ground, fight." An ambush certainly meets that criteria.

The basic counter ambush immediate action drill is to attack in the direction of the ambush. Never seek concealment. Never move away. Return massive amounts of fire. Assault the ambushers with extreme aggression and tenacity. The rationale for this tactic is that you are in a "kill zone", and the only area not in the kill zone is the ambusher's position. Ambushes are initiated to kill you. Your only chance for survival is to fight your way out.

A counter-sniper immediate action drill should be developed. Operators should be trained to take evasive measures, direct counter-sniper fire, and clear danger areas. The purpose of a sniper is to inflict casualties, create confusion, demoralize, harass, channel, provide fire support, select and remove targets, and observe and report. The best tactic when engaged by a sniper is to take cover behind an object that will stop a high powered rifle. Telephone poles and trees less than one foot in diameter will not stop .308 and .223 caliber bullets. The best cover would be brick walls, car engine blocks, and mounds of dirt three feet thick. Cement block constructed walls may not stop rifle fire. Move quickly from one cover position to another. Never move in a straight line. Move in short bursts in a random pattern. Build up a steady rate of fire while maneuvering towards the sniper.

Another successful technique for exiting the danger area is called the "Peel Back". The lead man aggressively steps forward and empties his weapon in the direction of the hostile fire. When he has expended all rounds in his weapon, he steps aside, allowing the second man to commence the same procedure. The lead man goes to the rear, seeks cover and concealment, and reloads his weapon; maintaining a posture to return covering fire for the rest of his team.

The second man does the same as the lead man, takes up a similar position of advantage and reloads his weapon. The remainder of the team executes the same tactic and the procedure is used until the entire team is out of the danger area and in a position of safety.

The team should have a tactic to extract a man down outside of a structure that is in the "kill zone" and hostile fire is a threat or is continuing. In lieu of an armored vehicle, especially if time is critical; and it usually is, ballistic vests can be placed on the roof and windows of a four door vehicle. Remove the back seat. Drive between the aggressor and the injured operator. A second man in the rear opens the rear door and pulls the injured operator into the vehicle. The vehicle drives out of the kill zone. If necessary, cover fire can be incorporated.

There are three basic immediate action drills for a man down after entry: (1) the next man in line steps forward and returns fire. The second man pulls the downed operator to safety, (2) two operators step forward to return fire and the third man pulls the downed operator to safety, and (3) the assault team continues the assault calling in perimeter security/trailers to extract the wounded operator. All team members should carry a compress bandage on their person in the same place. When treating a wounded operator, use his bandage to treat him. It is suggested that every team member be trained in first aid. Paramedics and TEMS are also highly recommended to be included as members of the team.

It should be pre-determined what action will be taken if the assault results in a hostage situation. This, obviously, is a very fluid and dynamic situation and most likely the decision will be made by the Team Leader when it occurs. Options to consider are: (1) contain and call out, (2) negotiate, (3) sniper option, (4) deploy CS or OC (5) covert/stealth entry, and (6) dynamic assault.

Many times there are hostages taken or transported from the original hostage scene in vehicles. For this immediate action drill scenario an automobile is the target conveyance. Practice is essential for the success of this type of operation. The assault team should be no more than 10 seconds away from the target vehicle. There should be designated shooters and designated hostage handlers. A diversion is essential. Head shots are recommended. Hand guns can be used because of the extremely close range. The effect of glass on the trajectory of the bullet must be taken into consideration, especially the windshield which deflects the round downward, sometimes as much a six inches. Side windows shatter. Rear windows become opaque after being impacted by one round. The best shooting positions are through the side windows and by placing the muzzle of the pistol as near as possible to the windshield to avoid deflection. It is recommended to aim high on the forehead in a windshield shot. Remember the effects of projectiles through glass called "spalling". Particles of glass fly out in a cone shaped pattern at the same velocity as the bullet and can kill or wound the suspect and/or hostage. Designated hostage handlers yell to the hostage by name, if known, to come to them and quickly take them out of the field of fire. If the hostage freezes, the handler must extract him from the vehicle. Further vehicle assault tactics will be discussed in Chapter 16 "Mobile Arrest/Vehicle Assault".

CHAPTER 7

Live Fire Training

The average police gun battle is over in 2.1 seconds with two or three shots fired in dim or dark conditions at seven yards or less (half were five feet or less). Most departments' firearms qualifications do not match the statistics of an encounter. The average police officer qualifies at night every five years. The military has renewed the emphasis of Close Quarter Battle (CQB) since the invasion of Panama and retaking of Kuwait City. A post combat analysis led to the realization that the effective employment of surgical forces in an urban environment was necessary.

The purpose of live fire training is to teach CQB tactics utilizing reactive aimed fire for Aimed Quick Kills (AQK). The course commences with an overview, safety, and administrative guidelines. A general outline would include weapons' familiarization, principles of combat marksmanship, weapons zero, reactive shooting (AQK), CQB dry fire, simunitions (marker round) drills, and CQB live fire.

Live fire training is not qualification and should be supervised by Range Safety Officers (RSOs) that are proficient with firearms and have expertise in CQB. Weapons handling, range control, and target placement are paramount safety issues. The inherently hazardous nature of CQB requires strict attention to detail from all participants. Two RSOs should be present for large multi-room scenarios. RSOs will ensure that all participants are thoroughly briefed. RSOs do not participate. They are responsible for the safety of the training. All participants will be equipped with body armor, eye and ear protection, and gloves.

Shooting houses with overhead observation walkways will require one RSO as an observer and the other RSO will follow the team into the structure. Loaded weapons are not authorized on the overhead observation platform. Targets will be placed to ensure the safety of all personnel in adjacent rooms and outside the house (range fan). The RSO setting up the targets will have the second RSO double-check target placement.

A medical technician will be present at all times. If two medics are present, both may participate in the training. A single medic will remain in a safe position that ensures minimum risk of injury. The medic will ensure those necessary items to treat trauma including IV solution and oxygen are present at the sight. Each participant will carry a battle dressing in a designated pocket in his uniform, or load-bearing equipment, which will be used by the medic in case of injury. This should be SOP for the team. Medical considerations will be covered in the safety brief to include treatment responsibilities, location of the nearest hospital, and MEDEVAC plan.

Commands to be used on the site will include, but are not limited to, the following:

"Cease Fire" - The single most important command. All firing will cease on this command. If initiated by someone other than the RSO, the RSO will immediately take control of the situation.

"The Range Is Cold" - The RSO will declare the range "Cold". All firing will immediately halt and weapons secured.

"The Range is Hot" - When the range is safe and ready the RSO will declare the range "hot"

"Down Range" - This is declared by anyone moving down range after the range has been called "Cold" by the RSO. The command "Down Range" will be repeated by everyone on the range. This will confirm that everyone is aware someone is going down range and lets the man going down range know that everyone is aware.

To enter a room declare "Coming In" and wait for the reply "Come In". To leave a room, or the shooting house, declare "Coming Out" and wait for the reply "Come Out".

"Clear" - When the room/space is clear and secure

"Moving" - Operator wants to move

"Move" - Acknowledgment of the operator's moving request, granting him permission to move.

"Stand Fast" - Stop what you are doing and stand by for further instructions.

"Check" - This is called only after the room is clear when the primary weapon has run dry, or is jammed, and you are on your secondary weapon. The verbal "check" is called out, followed by an "OK" from your partner. Upon hearing the "OK" reply, you immediately re-holster your secondary weapon and attend to your primary weapon. When the primary weapon is on line, bring it to the contact ready position and give the verbal "Ready". This signifies to your partner that movement can continue and his response is once again "OK".

"Cover" - is called when the primary and secondary weapons are down while dropping to one knee. Stay on one knee until the verbal "Covering" is heard. Correct the problem, then give the verbal "Ready" before standing up.

"Hot" - is called when overwhelmed in a room and reinforcements are needed. The next numbered shooters in line immediately enter and engage targets. (ie: hot 4 - next four shooters dynamically enter the room). When the last room is clear, the team leader declares the structure clear and announces "Team Coming Out". The RSO authorizes the action by the verbal "Come Out".

Weapons should be zeroed at different ranges to determine points of impact/point of aim variations. Accuracy drills utilizing two inch circles that are numbered can develop accuracy and target discrimination skills. Target boards displaying different geometric shapes and different colored balloons are also effective in discrimination drills. It is suggested to start slow and increase speed to develop skill and confidence. Practice half speed, then three quarters, and then full speed.

Marksmanship fundamentals should be stressed to include stance, grip, sight flash, breath control, and trigger control. Shooting inside of 25 yards should be with both eyes open. Cellophane tape applied to shooting glasses over the non-dominant eye can help develop this capability. Aimed fire with one eye closed is recommended outside 25 yards. The finger is always outside the trigger guard until the sight flash is acquired and the shot is taken. The "low ready" position with the weapon pointed down at a 45-degree angle and "contact ready" position with the muzzle of the weapon about one inch below the line of sight are recommended CQB weapons handling techniques. The "high ready" is not recommended for CQB.

Once accuracy and weapons handling skills are at a satisfactory level, shooting on the move is commenced. This can be conducted from either the "Isosceles" or "Modified Weaver". Accuracy is important, not the stance. The best success is achieved by moving in a crouch with knees bent, shoulders level, and weapon at "contact ready". Students move forward in a line and fire on command. Particular attention is necessary from the RSOs to ensure a shooter does not get in front or behind the firing line.

The "immediate threat" concept is drilled where the shooter immediately aggresses and engages a target. The shooter is required to engage the threat and neutralize it with AQK in less than 1.5 seconds. Lateral movement drills, shooting while moving backwards, and team drills are next

When the shooters have achieved satisfactory skills, they then engage moving targets and then moving targets while moving. Drills for shooting on the move to cover, reloading, and shooting on the move to another position of cover are recommended. Steel targets give "instant gratification" when hit, but you must be aware of a splash back at close range. Reactive targets with balloons in them also give reality to live fire drills especially three dimensional targets that train the shooter to place shots at angles that hit vital organs or center brain. A non-fatal hit, or hit that will be fatal in the future, is not the objective of AQK.

Shooting with ballistic shields, especially "lipping" around door frames to give maximum protection and "slicing the pie" are good drills. Drug Influence/Body Armor immediate action drill ("Mozambique") is a good failure drill when the aggressor does not go down after the first volley. The shooter immediately takes a head shot. This drill gives the shooter the confidence to take an initial head shot.

"Stacking Guns" is a technique for maximizing fire power around a corner or down a hallway. The first shooter takes an

L-shaped prone position around a corner. The second man takes a squatting or kneeling position over the prone shooter. The third man stands over the two. This "stacks" three weapons to concentrate fire.

Malfunction and reload drills with SMG, shotgun, and pistol should be an integral part of CQB training. Remember "Murphy's Laws":

Murphy's Laws

1. If the enemy is within range, then so are you.

2. If you're short of everything but the enemy, then you are in the combat zone.

3. The easy way is always mined.

4. In war, important things are simple and simple things are hard.

5. Communications will fail as soon as you need fire support desperately.

6. No OPLAN survives first contact intact.

7. There is no such thing as a perfect plan.

Murphy provides you with bad intelligence, breaks your equipment, and jams your weapons. Murphy is always there. Going into combat is extremely stressful and causes predictable reactions in operators. They forget how to perform the simplest tasks under pressure unless they are drilled in them repeatedly.

When a long gun malfunctions, squeeze the trigger twice, and if it does not fire, transition to your secondary weapon immediately. The failure drill for a handgun is to squeeze the trigger twice, and if there is no secondary weapon:

> SLAP - the magazine
>
> RACK- the slide back
>
> ENGAGE- the target

Most malfunctions are caused by an empty or unseated magazine. "Stove Pipes" (casing stuck in a chamber) can be cleared by holding the weapon in your strong hand and chopping backward with your other hand to dislodge the casing. A failure to extract or double feed is cleared by removing the magazine and inverting the pistol and racking the slide back one or two times. Reload and engage.

When clearing a weapon verbalize by yelling "Cover". The partner yells " Covering". When the weapon is back in battery, yell "Ready", and the partner yells "OK". A procedure should be developed where verbalizations are automatic and simple. It is best not to have more than one meaning for a command. For example, if you use "Clear" in a malfunction drill, you might not want to use "Clear" to announce a room has been cleared. Murphy is waiting. Verbalizations can be confused under stress and with diversionary devices, weapons fire, wounded people, glass breaking, dust, smoke and the routine CQB environment confusion should be avoided as much as possible.

Start slowly and allow the team to gain confidence. Practice shooting standing, kneeling, speed kneeling, squatting, prone, L-shaped prone, on the back, sitting, moving, from cover, around corners, stepping over a downed partner, "stacked guns" and then put on gas masks and do it again.

The operator must be able to maximize his effectiveness during dim light and darkness. To see in the dark he must understand how the eye is constructed. The lens focuses light just as the lens of a camera. The iris regulates the amount of light. The retina corresponds to the film in the camera and transmits images to the brain. The retina is composed of cone cells and rod cells. Cone cells allow you to see colors and require a great deal of light. They are your day eyes. They are concentrated directly behind the lens and decrease in number from the center. Rod cells produce a chemical substance called visual purple which makes them active in darkness and low illumination. They are your night eyes, and allow you to distinguish between black and white and shades of gray. Most rod cells are in the area of the retina.

It takes about 30 minutes for your eyes to become accustomed to low levels of illumination because the rod cells produce visual purple. Off center vision allows you to focus on an object without looking directly at it so the image is formed in rod cells that are sensitive in darkness. Visual purple bleaches out in four to ten seconds so it is necessary to scan your eyes back and forth over the object. Night vision is destroyed quickly by bright light. If this cannot be avoided, close one eye to preserve night vision in that eye. In summary, for night vision, look slightly away from the object, scan back and forth, and avoid bright lights.

All weapons should be equipped with lights. In the absence of this equipment, hand held illumination tactics have been developed. The "Chapman" technique for handguns uses a flashlight in the weak hand holding it palm down, thumb toward the body. The backs of the hands are together for isometric pressure. The light is turned on only for target identification and to allow sight flash.

In the absence of lights, night sights are the best option. However, many departments will not allow their officers to have night sights on their hand guns. Tactics have been developed, out of necessity, using the above night vision principles and firing at center mass with both eyes open to maximize night vision. They protect their night vision as best as possible. One muzzle flash reduces night vision. Recovery is about one minute.

CQB was devised for team assaults in confined space. There are two main doctrines that have emerged: (1) Speed, Surprise, Aggression (Violence of Action) and (2) Speed, Surprise and Diversion. Both doctrines stress rehearsals.

Surprise is the paramount objective. The team needs the lag time/reaction time to make entry. Surprise is gained through extensive planning based on scouting. Rehearsal of the entry is essential to success. Surprise can be the result of a diversion. Furthermore, judicious use of noise flash devices (NFDs) can be used after the breach is made to maximize on the surprise factor.

Speed allows the assault team to maximize on the results of surprise and diversion. The few seconds of lag time serves as security for the breaching phase. Speed of movement is accomplished in a "careful hurry", knees bent, shoulders level, weapon at "contact ready" both eyes open, and weapon pointing where you are looking. You should not move faster than you can engage targets for AQK. If all the targets are engaged and eliminated immediately upon entry, the principal of speed has been followed. But, if the assaulters move too quickly and fail to engage all targets, miss a target, or hit hostages or friendlies, the principle of speed has been violated.

Aggression or violence of action can be described as a sudden explosion of force that dominates the room and eliminates the threat. This, coupled with speed enables the assault team to maintain their element of surprise. Aggressive action is not limited to firepower. It is also a mental condition, a mind set, that lends to the command presence that results in dominating the situation. Threats are engaged by moving toward them and verbalized commands are simple and loud: "Police, Get Down. Get Down."

Diversions can be induced psychologically, by ruse, or by an action that will draw the aggressor's attention away from the breach point such as a diversionary device, fire extinguisher, or other distraction. This enables the assaulters to achieve entry successfully without being engaged. Once the element of surprise is lost (usually 3-5 seconds), the assault should switch from dynamic to another technique, unless it is a hostage rescue operation.

The principles of room entry are room domination, threat elimination, control of situation/personnel, and search for people or material. The size of the room will determine the number of assaulters. Most rooms require two assaulters. Dry fire entries should be drilled, starting slowly, to allow the operators to become accustomed to entering the breach point, getting out of the "fatal funnel" and moving quickly without sacrificing accuracy. Target placement is critical to avoid cross fires. Weapons handling should be emphasized. Points of domination and interlocking and collapsible fields of fire should be rehearsed.

The "fatal funnel" is caused by restricted vision going through a doorway. The suspect inside the room knows where the door is and has only one place to look. An assaulter must get through the doorway quickly. This is accomplished by placing the foot closest

DYNAMIC ROOM CLEARING
"FATAL FUNNEL"

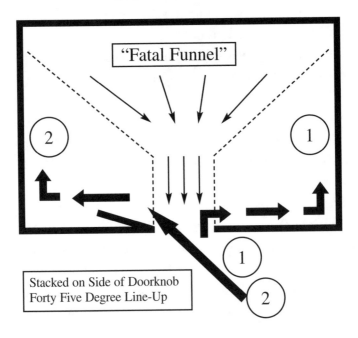

"Fatal Funnel"

Stacked on Side of Doorknob
Forty Five Degree Line-Up

to the wall forward and stepping through the doorway with the other foot. The next step takes you out of the fatal funnel.

The "button hook" is executed by an assaulter on each side of the door. The Point Man enters first and the Back Up second.

In the "criss cross" one assaulter goes high and the other low entering the room in different directions. The Point Man is first, but the execution is close to simultaneous.

In the "Snake" entry the Point Man does not have a predetermined entry and the Back Up enters in the opposite direction of his partner.

Room clearing can be executed a number of ways. The assaulters can "run the walls" and clear the contour of the room coming around toward the center, lowering their weapons to a low ready as they approach each other. Another technique is for the Point Man to go to the farthest corner on his half of the room while the Back Up man goes to the nearest corner. Each man clears visually always pointing his weapon where he is looking to one yard from the muzzle of his partner and back. He then points his weapon to the center of his area of responsibility and focuses his attention to the area. This is called "interlocking and collapsible fields of fire". Another entry method is the "limited penetration" technique where the entry team stops after initial entry and visually clears the room by the interlocking fields of fire method. A four-man entry team would be in a convex configuration with the number three and four men not as deep as one and two. This is not only an effective room domination technique, but a safe way to conduct live fire training.

It is recognized that making live fire training realistic and safe is difficult. Training should be conducted fully equipped, all evolutions repeated with gas masks, and in all weather and light conditions. Stress safety and the basics every time. Maximize your training time. There is no early end of watch. Remember Murphy.

Live Fire Training Sacon Shooting House

Live Fire Training Sacon Shooting House

Live Fire Vehicle Dismount

Live Fire Vehicle Dismount

Live Fire Training Range Shooting In Pairs

Live Fire Training Range Shooting In Pairs

CHAPTER 8

Shooting House
Construction

The reason most departments do not have shooting houses is because of the administrative impediments not the cost. First you must have land that is not zoned residential or has other covenants that will preclude construction. In addition to the noise factor, there might be another ordinance about noise at night. You might not be in an FAA approved area to conduct helicopter operations. The EPA might charge that the lead will contaminate the ground water. Mining the lead from shooting range berms can be expensive. Remember the Marplots. They will come out in full force to stop shooting house construction. The "experts" will disagree on how it should be built. Your Administration Section will gloomily announce that there is "no money". I have seen people disobey direct orders when it came to supporting shooting house construction or tactical training. One manager told me he was "philosophically opposed" to tactical training. Another said he felt the training during the academy was sufficient for the rest of an agent's career.

You can convert a range into a shooting house configuration using landscaping mesh or cheese cloth stapled to two-by-four studs to form a room. The entry point should be where the rounds will go down range and target placement should be in safe locations to avoid cross fires. One wall with a doorway and a blast wall can be constructed out of four-by-fours or railroad ties. The rest of the room can be constructed with landscaping mesh. Wires run across the top parallel and diagonally will support hanging targets such as balloons and three dimensional reactive targets.

Steel targets for CQB training are not encouraged because of the potential of splash back. Bullet traps made from armor plate lined with conveyor belt and/or "Linotex" can be made. Linotex is a brand name of a material that is self sealing. It is used to line the fuel tanks of fighter planes and race cars. Hand carts make good platforms for bullet traps and provide mobility. Two inch edges welded around the armor plate will prevent shrapnel from spraying out of the side. The larger 30 by 60 inch bullet traps are angled to deflect the shrapnel downward into a tray. They are also edged in conformation with the angle of the plate to form a box like structure.

Berms can be built and supported with plywood lined with Linotex to keep the dirt and sand from spilling out the bullet holes. Berms should be at least three feet thick to stop rifle ammunition.

"Tire Houses" constructed of tires filled with sand with overlapping columns and blast walls outside entry points were one of the first shooting house configurations used by DELTA, SEAL Team - 6, and HRT. Tire companies will give used tires away to save them the cost of disposal. Tires should be the same size to prevent a round from getting through the barrier. Also, the tires must be filled completely, or a round can hug the contour of the tire, exit the other side, and retain dangerous velocity.

There is a compound made from "Kevlar" (body armor

material) and recycled rubber bonded in strands to stop ricochets. Hardened steel is lined with this material to construct shooting house walls. A four inch circle will withstand up to five hundred rounds before the replacement of the panel is necessary. Titanium "popper" targets lined with this material are also available.

There is a material called shock attenuating concrete (SACON) that is a mixture of polypropylene fiber and concrete that can be poured into forms to build shooting houses. A six inch circle on a six inch thick wall will withstand up to 1,000 rounds. The compound will withstand up to .223 caliber rounds. A special pour that induces air into the mixture to make the compound more porous is used. Joint Task Force Six (JTF-6) constructed a SACON shooting house for DEA Los Angeles at the Los Angeles Sheriff's range. LAPD SWAT constructed bullet traps. JTF-6 also constructed a range and DEA installed computerized pop up, turning, and running targets. A reactive range was constructed out of railroad ties and landscape mesh to practice AQK. Rifle platforms were constructed. A 50 foot trailer was converted into a classroom, another trailer was used for storage, and a container was purchased for storage. Portable toilets were rented. This compound has been used since 1991 by many law enforcement and military teams with excellent results.

If your team conducts drug raids, you will qualify for assistance from JTF-6 in shooting house, range, helicopter pad, rapelling tower, and other drug enforcement related construction. Your department is responsible for any zoning compliance, building site, and material. The labor and equipment rental is provided by JTF-6. Additional sources of support are the National Guard and Army Corps of Engineers. The total cost for the DEA compound was approximately $40,000. Warriors - 1. Marplots - 0.

Live Fire Shooting House Constructed of Tires Filled With Sand

Sacon Shooting House Financed by DEA Los Angeles. Built by JTF-6/ Army Corps of Engineers on Los Angeles County Sheriff's Firearms Range

Armor Plate Bullet Trap Linotex Lining Prevents Splash Back

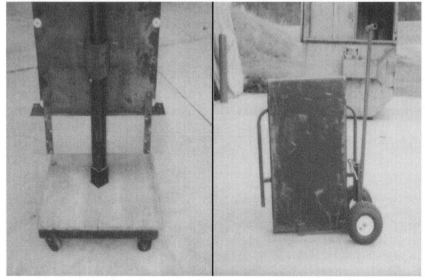

Armor Plate Linotex Lining Hand Cart

CHAPTER 9

Camouflage

The key to preventing detection of your location is to pay attention to the principals of camouflage and stealth movement. Remember: Silhouette, Shape, Shine, and Smell. If you look at the terrain in which you will be operating, you can determine the type of background you want to blend into by giving it a number. Black would be 100, and white would be zero. For example: in dense jungle, you would assign the background an 80 or 90 with most colors being black or dark green. In the snow, you would assign a low number depending upon other factors such as rocks, trees, or bushes. The key is to eliminate the silhouette and make your image flat against the background with no shape.

Mesh suits and ghille suits worn by snipers use three dimensional material with colors compatible with the terrain to give depth and shadows to eliminate the silhouette.

Many military units prefer to operate at night, because it makes detection of their movement difficult. SWAT and hostage rescue units often assault at BMNT (Beginning Morning Nautical Twilight - one half hour before dawn). This is when a suspect is in his deepest sleep, or at least has reduced reactions.

At night, hearing replaces the loss of visibility. Operators should stop and listen and be familiar with the sounds, sights, and smells in the area. Make sure equipment is packed properly and does not rattle or squeak. Hoods on parkas reduce visibility and hearing. Waterproof clothing tends to rustle and shine. Inspect all metal, including jacket zippers, to ensure they do not shine.

Objects are more visible on the skyline, so avoid being silhouetted on the skyline or tops of buildings. Noise discipline and light discipline are essential. Pass orders and information in a very quiet whisper. Use simple signals. Avoid open areas. Stop often and scan the area and listen.

Camouflage of the face and hands is important. Dark colors on prominent features such as nose, chin, cheek bones, and eyebrows are recommended. Put light colors on non-angular or soft surfaces. Remember the ears and back of the neck. An uncamouflaged face or hand can be seen at 1,000 yards.

Your smell can give you away. Cologne, toothpaste, mouthwash, soap, alcohol, tobacco, deodorant and diet are factors. If smell could be a factor, move to face the wind to avoid possible detection.

There are many examples of the use of camouflage in military operations. In Vietnam, particular attention was paid during patrol operations and ambushes. In the Falklands War, the British forces attacked almost exclusively at night when it was determined that the Argentinians were not as well-trained for night fighting.

The following is an excerpt on camouflage taken from a "Tactics International" Manual instructed by retired LASD/SEB Sergeant Gary Rovarino:

I. CAMOUFLAGE - DEFINITION

   A. A means of concealment that creates the effect of being part of the natural surroundings.

      1. More than careful use of color and surroundings

         a. Common sense

         b. Blend with surroundings

      2. Types of camouflage

         a. Contrast

         b. Color

         c. Texture

         d. Outline of silhouette

         e. Deception

      3. Traditional colors and patterns are not necessarily the best.

         a. Studies indicate 50% of males have some sight color deficiency.

         b. The Germans used shades of gray effectively during World War II.

         c. The Japanese effectively used varying shades of tan and gray in the jungles.

         d. Color spectrum ranges from white, absence of color to black, the total density of all colors.

         e. If light is diminished, man only sees colors as shades of gray.

            1) Difficult to distinguish colors

         f. Two points of nature:

            1) There are few straight lines.

            2) Only man walks upright with distinct movements.

               a) Must eliminate straight lines and outlines

               b) Movement must be controlled

               c) Faces are solid colors

                  (1) Both black and white

g. Tone down skin

   1) Contrast between skin, face, hands and environment must be reduced.

      (a) Natural materials can be used

      (b) Various camouflage paints probably best for a variety of reasons.

      (c) Procedure is simple

         (1) Shine areas are the forehead, cheek bones, nose and chin.

            • These areas should have dark colors

         (2) Shadow areas are around the eyes, under the nose and chin, and along with other exposed area.

            • Should use light colors for these areas

      (d) Use irregular patterns

      (e) Mesh net is used to break up the outline

4. Clothing

   a. Various types of camouflage

   b. Utilities and hats

   c. Use props

5. Weapons

   a. Straight lines

   b. Distinctive shapes

      1) Use tape

      2) Various paints are available

         a) Available at hobby shops, gray, flats, primer

         b) Make sure smells evaporate

      3) Burlap and cloth

         a) Use shades of gray, etc.

6. Equipment

    a. Check for light reflection objects.

    b. Flashes of light are almost always from man-made objects.

    c. Tape swivels and noise producers.

    d. Straps

II. PRINCIPLES OF CAMOUFLAGE

A. Make sure position is not occupied by suspects

B. Must offer concealment

    1. Background must absorb elements of the position.

C. Make every effort not to change the appearance of the background.

D. Position must not hinder the mission.

E. Use of most natural position is desirable.

F. Isolated landmarks such as trees, bushes, etc. should be avoided because they attract attention.

G. Use terrain irregularities, even though cover is scarce.

III. CAMOUFLAGE DISCIPLINE

A. Daytime

    1. Avoid activity that changes the appearance of the area.

    2. Only good as long as it is maintained

        a. Avoid breaking limbs, twigs, and vegetation.

            1) It becomes obvious to suspects familiar with the area.

            2) Do not smoke

        b. If you deploy at night you may have to move when more light becomes available.

    3. Nighttime

        a. Concealment at night is less necessary.

            1) Use cover of darkness to your advantage.

b. Light discipline is very important at night.

c. If you deployed in the daytime you may have to move at night.

d. Do not smoke

e. Noise discipline is especially important at night.

   1) Noise is intensified at night.

   2) Whispering should be avoided.

4. Camouflage construction should be avoided if at all possible.

a. Difficult to match existing area

b. Noticeable to persons familiar with the area

5. Blend natural material with artificial

6. Methods of camouflage

a. Hiding - Total and complete concealment

b. Blending - The arrangement of camouflage materials on, over, and around the individual and his equipment so as to appear to be part of the background

7. Deception

a. Making something appear to be something else.

IV. PRINCIPLES OF INDIVIDUAL CAMOUFLAGE

A. Concealment

1. Remain as motionless as possible

2. Use all available concealment

a. Always act as if you are being watched.

3. Take personal comfort into consideration.

4. Expose no reflective objects.

5. Blend

6. Check for back lighting.

7. Observe around or through objects rather than over them.

V. CAMOUFLAGE UNIFORMS

  A. Best known

    1. Jungle rip stop - woodland camouflage

      a. Wears out fast

      b. Fades easily - takes protection

      c. Wash cold water and dry with low heat

  B. New woodland green

    1. Heavier - reinforced

    2. Will shrink and fade

    3. May be hot in summertime or warm climates

  C. Desert cammies

    1. Southwest desert area of USA

  D. Night linear

    1. 3/16" squares and splotches

    2. Works well in defeating infrared and night viewing devices

  E. Solid gray utilities

    1. Is no better than faded green color at night

    2. Has advantages in daylight in urban surroundings

  F. Urban cammies

    1. Utilized basic woodland pattern but with black, gray, and white patterns.

    2. Best when configured in the "tiger stripe" pattern

CHAPTER 10

Hand Signals

Although communications technology has advanced considerably, occasionally radios malfunction or cannot be used during a critical phase of movement where command and control is essential. A few basic hand gestures will offer reasonable communications where no communication at all could easily cause an aborted or an unsuccessful mission. An operator should be able to resolve a communication situation and successfully communicate with team members. The following are suggested hand signals:

Prone Out
Hold arm out in vertical position, palm outstretched and down. Move hand and arm downward to indicate lowering position.

Put On Gas Mask

Open hand, place over mouth and nose.

Command of Execution

Hold arm out and vertical at elbow.
Move down in vertical direction.

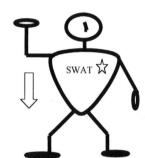

Weapon Malfunction

Thumb down sign over weapon

Room/Area Clear

Arm extended, hand in fist, thumb up

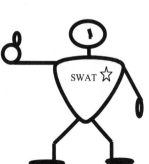

Search Room/Area
Hold arm across chest and extend
arm pointing to room/area you
want searched.

Take Over
Hold arm horizontally across chest,
hand extended palm down. Move
arm horizontally at waist level

Location of Suspect
Extend arm horizontally with
hand extended and fingers spread

Hurry Up
Hold out arm horizontally and
vertical at elbow, fist palm out,
motion rapidly, vertical up and down

Information
Hold hand and forearm in vertical position so that hand and forearm form letter "I"

Order
Hold forearm in vertical position, fist clenched, indicating firm order

Question
Hold forearm in vertical position, hand curved to form question mark

"YOU"
Hold arm outstretched and point index finger at receiving operator

HEAR

Hold hand in vertical position
behind ear

COME

Hold hand and arm outstretched; then
pull hand and forearm towards body
indicating movement towards yourself

THERE

Hold hand and arm out-
stretched pointing index finger
at object

NUMBERS

Numbers of persons or objects can
be indicated by holding the appropriate number of fingers erect

MESSAGE RECEIVED
Hold the hand and arm out-stretched touching tips of index finger and thumb together

UNABLE TO UNDERSTAND

DISREGARD LAST SIGNAL/PHRASE
Hold hand in front, palm out, move side to side

SUSPECT
Grasp wrist of other hand, hold as if taking suspect

ADULT

Arm and hand outstretched
above shoulder

"STOP"

Hold arm outstretched with
palm facing receiving operator

"GO"

Hold arm to form "L", swing arm from
rear indicating forward movement

"SEE" OR "WATCH"

Hold hand parallel against
forehead over eyes

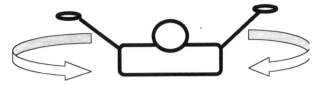

ENTER
Hold hands
and arms outstretched,
rotate arms rearward as if parting curtains

AROUND
Usually used with go,
hand turned at angle

GET OR OBTAIN
Used in conjunction with go, make
a fist as if grasping object

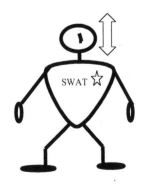

YES
Rotate head up and down

NO
Rotate head side to side

"ME" OR "MYSELF"
Point the index finger of the
hand at the center of your chest

JUVENILE
Hold arm and hand outstretched
below shoulder height

FEMALE
Hold fists against chest indicating
breasts or female gender

MALE
Stroke cheek downward motion indicating beard or male gender

POLICEMAN OR BACK UP OFFICER
Point and touch badge

SERGEANT OR FIELD SUPERVISOR
Hold three fingers on opposite arm indicating three (3) stripes

WINDOW
With index fingers, Outline window by starting at top center and extending out and down

DOOR

With index fingers, outline door
by starting at top center and
extending out and down

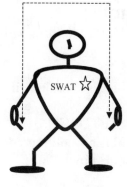

AUTOMOBILE

Hold both fists in front of body, make
half circle motion as if steering

SHIP

Make motion of vessel on waves

PISTOL

Move finger like pulling trigger

RIFLE
Motion holding rifle

SMG
Motion holding rifle, rapidly move trigger finger

SHOTGUN
Motion holding rifle, moving hand as if
pumping shotgun

OUT OF AMMUNITION
Motion with hand across throat

INJURED
Make chopping motion
where you are injured

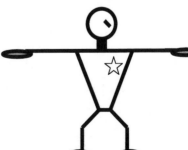

AIRPLANE
Hold arms out as wings

HELICOPTER
Simulate rotor blade over head

HOSTAGE
Hold arm with other hand

TRAINING AID

Below is a list of commonly used gestures, which can be used as a training aid:

A. ORDERS

"YOU COME HERE"

"YOU STOP THERE"

"YOU GO THERE"

"YOU GO AROUND THERE"

"YOU GO GET SHOTGUN"

"YOU GO GET SERGEANT"

"YOU GO GET TWO POLICEMEN"

"YOU GO AROUND THERE, WATCH DOOR"

"YOU GO AROUND THERE, WATCH WINDOW"

"YOU GO AROUND THERE, WATCH SUSPECT'S AUTO"

B. INFORMATION

"ONE SUSPECT THERE"

"TWO ARMED SUSPECTS THERE"

"THREE ADULT ARMED SUSPECTS THERE"

"FOUR ADULT ARMED SUSPECTS THERE"

"ONE MALE SUSPECT, ONE FEMALE SUSPECT THERE"

"ONE ADULT MALE SUSPECT, ONE JUVENILE FEMALE SUSPECT"

"ONE FEMALE HOSTAGE, ONE MALE SUSPECT THERE"

"ONE SUSPECT, MENTALLY DERANGED"

C. QUESTIONS

"YOU SEE SUSPECT?"

"YOU HEAR SUSPECT?"

"YOU SEE HOSTAGE?"

"YOU HEAR HOSTAGE?"

"YOU SEE SUSPECT'S AUTO?"

"SUSPECT ARMED?"

"ONE SUSPECT?"

"ADULT SUSPECT?"

"MALE SUSPECT?"

The above are suggested hand signals. Creativity and imagination will assist your team in developing their system of silent communication.

CHAPTER 11

Breaching Concepts

The most basic breaching technique is mechanical. A sledge hammer applied with enough force on or near a door knob will usually force a door open. A ram will do the same thing. A pick or hooligan tool tapped between the door and door jamb near the lock will allow leverage to "bow" the door with enough space to release the lock. It is important to remember to provide cover for the breacher and for the breacher to place the equipment outside and away from the breach point once the breach has been accomplished to avoid interference with the entry team. Hydraulic jacks or "Jamb Spreaders" exert many tons of pressure to allow entry. These are effective on more heavily constructed doors.

Exothermic Entry Torches cut steel bars in three seconds and door locks in seven seconds. They are quiet and portable enough to allow security during the breaching phase.

Shotgun breaching was initially developed using 10 gauge shotguns and shells reloaded with dental plaster. The problem with using conventional loads was the possible lethality due to impact after target penetration. The purpose of developing a frangible or disintegrating projectile was to provide a means of breaching the locking mechanism of the door with minimal "behind the target" effect. There are a number of commercially available shotgun breaching rounds available composed of zinc oxide powder, tungsten and copper powder, fine lead, metal slag and wax, fine steel powder, steel bird shot, ceramic and fine metal filings, and modeling clay mixed with fine metal powder. The shotgun must be equipped with an adaptor or modified barrel to prevent back pressure from exploding the barrel. The barrel should be held firmly against where the deadbolt and latch are in the door jamb. The barrel should be angled downward to prevent possible injury of a person standing near the door. The breach should be made with two simultaneous shots to assure successful destruction of the locking mechanisms. Breaching can also be accomplished by shooting the hinges. Again, the breacher should be covered at all times during the operation.

Explosive breaching has been part of the military inventory for decades. Civilian agencies have recently adopted this technique. The four primary explosive hazards are: heat, fragmentation, over pressure, and fumes. Nomex uniforms including balaclavas, eye and ear protection, ballistic helmets, and blast shields are required.

Charges should be constructed by an EOD technician. Secondary charges are recommended in the event the primary fails. Dual priming is recommended for a redundant back up system for ignition. The most common types of charges are: sheet explosives, primafoam, caulking, shape charges (designed to cut "Monroe Effect"), explosive tape, and conical charges.

An excellent book by Steven Mattoon, *Modern Explosive Breaching Techniques - A Guide for SWAT and Special Operations Personnel* published by VARRO PRESS provides an outline for developing this capability. Some of the areas covered are Detonating Cord (DET CORD) which are either PETN

(Pentaerythrite Tetranitrate) or RDX (Cyclonite) explosive filler. DET CORD is fabricated into breaching charges and can be placed into pre-fabricated frames. Explosive Cutting Tape (ECT) and Low Hazard Flexible Linear Shaped Charges (LHFLSC) have excellent breaching properties. ECT retains a high degree of flexibility after repeated deformations such as rolling up in back packs and rucksacks. It has self-adhesive tape for easy attachment to the target site, resists water and, in fact, can be used under water.

A Linear Shaped Charge (LSC) is an explosive encased in a metallic seamless sheath, and fabricated in continuous lengths shaped in the form in an inverted "V". The LSC uses a shaped charge that cuts the target to which it is affixed. It must be detonated from the apex of the shaped charge to preserve what is called the "Monroe Effect". The jetting effect of a shaped charge concentrates the explosive action through the use of the shaped charge.

Sheet Explosive is made of either RDX or PETN. Sheet explosive is held in high esteem by special operators for its ease of use, and placement in frames and on hard targets. Next to plastic, it is the most flexible and moldable high energy explosive. It is superb for breaching work.

It is highly recommended that all detonators should be Shock Tube (Nonel) type because of the electrical fields produced by radios, cell phones, and other electronic equipment. Initiators should be designed to interface with any Nonel Shock Tube system. There should be a primary and backup positive safety system. They should be durable and be able to be fired either by hand or foot.

Door breaching remains the primary means of entry for most raid teams. Charges have been fabricated to blow through wooden doors. A piece of cardboard is cut with DET CORD taped around the outside diameter. This device allows the operator to design the size of entry portal required. The explosion cuts a hole in the door in the shape of the DET CORD outline. The basic formula is to use 50 grain DET CORD - one wrap for hollow core, two wraps for particle filled, and three wraps for solid or heavier wood doors. There are pre-fabricated Wood Door Breaching Devices that concentrate the explosive on the space between the door knob and jamb. These devices result in minimal fragmentation. One of the most successful metal door breaching methods is the use of water charges. There are also pre-fabricated Metal Door Breaching Devices (MDBD) for fire doors, security doors, and metal encased wooden doors. Operators load the devices with explosives depending on the type of door. These devices are designed to limit fragmentation also. MDBD's can be linked to open metal doors that swing out towards the staging area.

Another basic entry option is through windows entailing glass breaching. The common method is "break and rake"; however, this is time consuming. Explosive breaching is faster, minimizes damage to the structure, and the over pressure with glass powder minimizes damage to the target area vice wood or steel fragments. There are pre-fabricated glass breaching devices on poles available on the market.

Breaching structures is a more sophisticated entry tactic because it requires that the breacher compute the "Load Data" to defeat the target site.

The advantages are:

1. Complete surprise

2. Allows team to enter at time and place of choosing

3. Allows team to enter close to hostages

4. Allows instant dominating position

Shaped charges with water are used to defeat walls. Scouting is essential to avoid rebar, gas service lines, plumbing lines, studs, electrical wiring, load bearing walls, and major furniture and appliances.

There is also a pre-fabricated "gunport frame" that will allow a breach that will provide an operator a field of fire from outside the structure to allow immediate and close support for the entry team.

Other types of breaching are through the roof, ceiling, and floor. There are also breaching devices for aircraft, marine, oil rigs, trains, and multistory vertical assault

There should be a pre-mission breacher's brief. The breacher is usually the second man in the line up behind the point man with the blast shield. After the charge is in place, the breacher returns to the number two position. After a "thumbs back/squeeze up" the charge is detonated and entry in initiated. Mechanical breaching tools should be at the set point in the event of a malfunction.

Teams have been encountering protective steel doors and bars on windows. Usually second story houses do not have bars on the second level and entry can be made at that level. A technique of pulling bars with vehicles has been developed. This usually involves ropes or cargo straps with pointed steel hooks to penetrate wire mesh. Most protective steel doors swing out and in the opposite direction of the door they protect.

At first, contract tow trucks were used, but this was not the best solution because they were noisy and cumbersome. More importantly, the civilian truck driver was exposed to danger. Departments developed their own techniques. Doors can be pulled in the direction that they open, or by placing one hook on the upper right and the other on the lower left with a shorter rope. This causes increased torque when pulled. One technique is to tie a 10 foot rope as a safety line to window bars to prevent the door from flying. The door and window bars have a tendency to swing in an arc and are extremely hazardous to the entry team.

Bars on windows are usually anchored to studs with the center bars often omitted. Hook the bars near anchor points and pull away from the anchor points across the window. Generally, the more sturdy the bars, the more completely they are removed.

Breaching walls can be accomplished using bar pull equipment. One technique is to pull out the window sill. This usually leaves a breach as large as a door.

Naturally, any breaching technique should be practiced and rehearsed. It is extremely stressful and frustrating for a team leader to watch operators struggle for an unanticipated period of time at the breach point. An alternate breach point should always be part of the OPLAN.

DOOR NOMENCLATURE

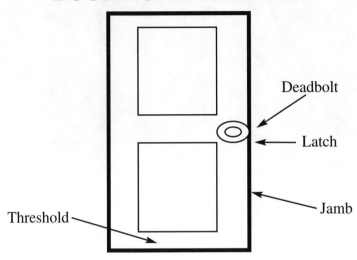

BREACHING DOORS

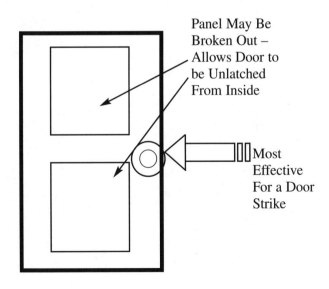

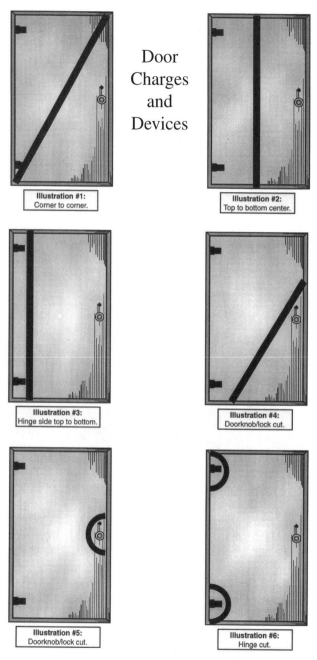

Door
Charges
and
Devices

Illustration #1:
Corner to corner.

Illustration #2:
Top to bottom center.

Illustration #3:
Hinge side top to bottom.

Illustration #4:
Doorknob/lock cut.

Illustration #5:
Doorknob/lock cut.

Illustration #6:
Hinge cut.

Illustrations courtesy of Steven Mattoon, *Modern Explosive Breaching Techniques*

STEEL BAR DOORS AND WINDOWS

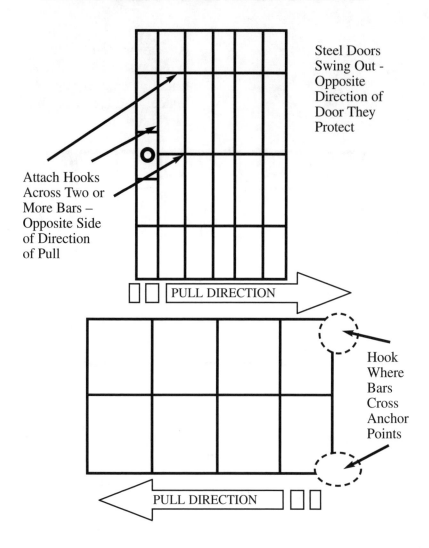

Steel Doors Swing Out - Opposite Direction of Door They Protect

Attach Hooks Across Two or More Bars – Opposite Side of Direction of Pull

PULL DIRECTION

Hook Where Bars Cross Anchor Points

PULL DIRECTION

BREACHING WALLS

Breaching Walls Near Windows & Doors Risks Encountering Smaller Spaces and Extra Framing Members

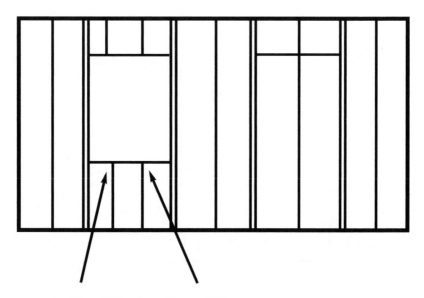

Pulling Window From Sill Often Tears Loose Studs Underneath – Can Create Opening Larger Than Door

Photos courtesy of Steven Mattoon, *Modern Explosive Breaching Techniques*

Photos courtesy of Steven Mattoon, *Modern Explosive Breaching Techniques*

CHAPTER 12

Less Lethal Weapons and Munitions

It is an accepted reality that specialized units are expected to be properly trained and equipped. They are held at a higher standard and are scrutinized much closer on their use of force. They are expected to reduce the potential for a lethal confrontation thus forcing commanders to make the critical decision to utilize less lethal weapons and munitions ranging from batons, to chemical munitions, noise flash devices, and kinetic energy weapons also called "long range impact weapons".

Most police agencies have a use of force continuum policy. It is recognized that a citizen is protected by the Fourth Amendment from unreasonable force. It is established doctrine that the force utilized to make an arrest must be reasonable and necessary. The use of force should be sufficient to end the confrontation. It is recommended that the appropriate amount of force be utilized to end the confrontation quickly. Extended encounters lead to increased potential for injuries on both sides.

One option is the use of impact force with a wooden baton or collapsible steel baton. One of the problems reported by instructors is lack of force and inaccurate targeting. This can be rectified with realistic training. A number of companies manufacture full protective gear to aid in this type of training to provide realism and assessment of the amount and accuracy of force applied.

Another tactic is called the "tangle team". Three officers grab the suspect's arms and legs and simply overpower and subdue the suspect. This is effective in demonstrations and "sit ins".

Chemical munitions are recommended when an entry is not the best option. The basic concept is space deprivation - making the enclosure uninhabitable for the suspect. Deployment of CS usually will force the suspect to exit the building and comply with commands over 75 percent of the time. Covert entry and direct application of CS or OC (oleoresin capsicum - derived from cayenne pepper) is an alternative option. This can be delivered from an aerosol container, launcher, or shotgun round.

Kinetic energy munitions are fired from shotguns or specialized launchers. The majority of the launchers are 37 millimeter. The objective of these rounds is to incapacitate the subject with a limited chance of significant injury or death.

The two main factors in the use of kinetic energy munitions are: shot placement/point of impact and the amount of energy transferred. It has been determined that generally, projectiles generating 120 to 160 foot-pounds of energy have the greatest potential for incapacitation with a minimal potential for causing serious injury or death when deployed at appropriate target areas. The operator will have to make that judgement based on his training and experience. For example, shot placement will vary based on the suspect's size and potential threat to the operator, civilians, or team members. The head and neck should be avoided unless a deadly force situation occurs. The chest and torso areas are effective. The abdominal area can cause damage to the liver, spleen, and kidneys.

Basic factors to consider are: need for the force, relationship between the need and the amount of force used, extent of injury inflicted, and whether the force was applied in a good faith effort to maintain order and restore public safety.

There have been five deaths in the United States and Canada as a result of the use of these munitions in the past 25 years. Two persons died from fractured ribs causing internal hemorrhage after being struck by launched projectiles. One person died after being struck in the throat by a launched projectile. Two persons were killed by shotgun launched "bean bag" rounds. The first was a non-penetrating impact on the sternum causing fatal cardiac arrhythmia. The second fatal incident was a result of penetration into the chest cavity of the "bean bag" round that lodged in the heart.

In the past, the plastic baton round was used most frequently followed by the 12 gauge "bean bag" round which was increasing in frequency of use. Currently the 12 gauge round is used slightly more than the baton round. In regards to injuries sustained, bruising was the most common with 53 percent, and abrasions accounted for 20 percent. About five percent incurred no injuries at all, and about four percent of the incidents involved lodging of the projectile under the suspect's skin.

Less lethal munitions are most utilized in incidents involving suicidal persons. This involves about 50 percent of the total incidents reported. "Suicide By Cop" incidents have increased, and extended range impact weapons are an effective tool to resolve these potentially dangerous situations. Barricaded suspects are the next most frequently reported incidents at 24 percent.

Law enforcement agencies in the Western United States represent the vast majority of reported usages of less lethal munitions with 59 percent. Southern states follow with 28 percent, followed by the Midwest at nine percent, and the Northeast with four percent of total incidents reported.

The San Diego P. D. established specialized teams called "Tactically Aggressive but Necessary Gambit of Options" (TANGO Teams) to respond to incidents that might occur during the last Republican Convention. Each team consisted of the Team Leader, apex man armed with a multiple round launcher, two shotgun men with "bean bag" rounds, two shield men carrying OC canisters, and two rifle men. The ninth man was the Sniper/Observer. The SDPD was able to field six TANGO Teams to support Mobile Field Force Platoons.

The utilization of less lethal munitions has evolved into an established part of the use of force policy and tactics. It is highly recommended that this be included in the development of a tactical team. All training should be documented.

CHAPTER 13

Diversionary Tactics and Devices

Diversion is defined as " a diverting or turning aside", a distraction of attention as a diversion from the enemy, anything that distracts or diverts attention. There are two categories of diversion: DECEPTIVE - something that deceives, as an illusion - also known as a psychological diversion, and PHYSIOLOGICAL - having to do with the functions of an organism.

Deceptive diversions require the suspect to draw an inference. For example, one tactical team posed as construction workers and started digging a trench in the suspect's front yard with a backhoe. When the suspect came out to complain, the "foreman" with clipboard in hand inquired as to the address, if it was the suspect's residence, and his identity. When the suspect identified himself, he was arrested without incident. Another example of a deceptive diversion is to phone the suspect with knowledge of the telephone's location. When the suspect answers, the team will have the opportunity to locate and isolate the suspect either by stealth or dynamic entry. Telephones can be used to convey the ruse that the suspect's demands have been met and "take him to the window" to observe a vehicle that has been negotiated. Further negotiations, entry, or the sniper option are possibilities.

There is a possibility that a psychological diversion will not work, because the suspect refuses to believe it. It is possible that the suspect could come to the wrong conclusion. Failure should be anticipated and a contingency plan should be formulated.

Physiological diversions function differently than psychological (deceptive) diversions in that they affect senses. Noise Flash Devices (NFDs) or Distraction Devices affect hearing, sight, and feeling - (an instantaneous increase and decrease in atmospheric pressure - over pressure and under pressure).

Noise Flash Devices made their debut in the tactical arena when counterterrorist units began using them in hostage rescue operations in the 1970's. The most famous was the Israeli hostage rescue operation at Entebbe airport in Uganda on July 3, 1976. This was followed by the German (GSG9) rescue of hostages from a Lufthansa airliner in Mogadishu, Somalia on October 18, 1977. British SAS rescued hostages from the Iranian Embassy at Princes Gate, London, England on May 5, 1980. The Swiss Group-De-Intervention Gendarmerie rescued hostages from the Polish Embassy in Bern, Switzerland in September 1982. NFDs then became "state of the art" for SWAT teams in the United States.

Specifications that are important for consideration when purchasing NFDs are the decibel level, candela output, and the fuse mechanism function. Decibels are sound measurement. It is accepted that an NFD should be at approximately 170dB. One hundred eighty five (185) dB is typically the threshold for ear damage. An example of 170 dB would be the sound of an M-16 rifle firing once from about five feet from your ear.

Candela is a standard for measuring light. Modern commercially manufactured NFDs emit approximately 2 million candela.

The most common fuse mechanism incorporates a bouchon, a ring with attached pin, and a "spoon". A cardboard body contains the charge. Fuses used in most NFDs are from the U.S. military M201-A1. The average firing time is 1.5 seconds.

The main types of canisters are: separating submunition allowing the bouchon to separate from the charge prior to ignition, the deflagrating canister which bursts or burns so that the bouchon is not propelled, and the non-bursting canister which is vented to allow for expansion of gases. The non-bursting canister has it's advantages in that it's weight allows it to be thrown through obstacles. The capability to penetrate glass is particularly effective for vehicular hostage rescue operations. There have been instances where injury has been incurred from the NFD body on ignition. Safety is a primary consideration in the deployment of NFDs.

There are single, double, and seven bang configurations available. Add on units for additional munitions, CS, and smoke are also on the market. Shotgun and other launchable devices are available. Consideration should be given to: range, delay time, and fire potential. NFD's can be equipped with command fire electric ignition for remote pre-placement. They can be attached to "painters' poles" or "flash sticks" for second story operations or through windows and crawl spaces.

Team members should be educated on the effects of NFDs. The basic purpose is to allow the team "lag time" to execute a tactic before the suspect recovers from the effects of the NFD. This is usually 5-8 seconds. During this time frame a number of dynamics occur. The suspect is exposed to over pressure and under pressure that the body cannot quickly adapt to. The loud 170dB impulse noise is disorienting and creates a stimulus that also must be adapted to. The 2 million candela flash bleaches a chemical in the eye called rhodopsin which temporarily interferes with vision. This will occur even if the eyelids are closed. A chemical called acetylcholine is secreted that induces a surrender response. This chemical is found in possums when they "play dead" and bears when they hibernate. These clinical effects are documented in court records.

In addition to documented training, it is essential that the department have a written policy. The SWAT Commander must be able to articulately testify as to why he authorized the NFD deployment. The written policy should specify who is authorized to deploy these devices. Training and refresher training should be available. Policy should allow discretion to deploy NFDs in emergency situations. When writing a policy there are several fundamental concepts which should be considered:

1. An NFD is not a substitute for good tactics

2. An NFD should not be used without justification

3. The device should be deployed by a designated trained operator only

4. Generally, the device should not be used solely for the preservation of evidence

Courts have upheld the use of diversionary devices and ruled that they do not violate the Fourth Amendment protection from unreasonable search and seizure. Most concern is raised in civil actions brought under 42 USC 1983 for excessive force.

One landmark case in the California Supreme Court (Langford v. Gates) challenged LAPD SWAT's use of a motorized battering ram and Noise Flash Device to serve a search warrant on a fortified "rock cocaine" house. The court ruled that magistrate review was necessary for the deployment of a motorized battering ram, but that such approval was not required for the use of diversionary devices because the LAPD had demonstrated well written policy and safe deployment procedures.

Any time there is an injury or potential for Fourth Amendment (use of force) and Fourteenth Amendment (due process) challenges, a department can expect to articulate why an NFD was deployed. A strategy is suggested to include:

1. Identify a court certified expert on NFDs

2. Have a written policy and adhere to it

3. Use appropriate terminology

An NFD is not a "grenade", "stun grenade", or "antiterrorist munition". The light emitted is bright, not "blinding". The sound is loud, not "deafening". NFDs ignite. They do not "detonate". They do not cause "panic", "fear", and "hysteria". They disorient, confuse, bewilder, and overwhelm the suspect with stimuli allowing him to be apprehended without being harmed.

Incidents of "suicide by cop" are increasing, and the deployment of NFDs is an option that might foil the attempt. One seasoned LASD SEB Team Leader put it succinctly: "We'll just continue their miserable lives a little bit longer. That's justice!"

LAPD/SWAT Break and Rake/NFD's

NOISE FLASH DEVICE
CUTAWAY VIEW

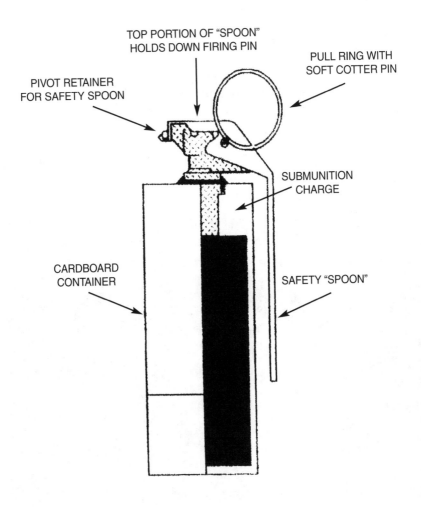

TOP PORTION OF "SPOON"
HOLDS DOWN FIRING PIN

PULL RING WITH
SOFT COTTER PIN

PIVOT RETAINER
FOR SAFETY SPOON

SUBMUNITION
CHARGE

CARDBOARD
CONTAINER

SAFETY "SPOON"

CHAPTER 14

Covert Audio and Visual Monitoring

Scouting the target location can give you a good idea of the floor plan and help you plan your entry, but it will not necessarily enable you to locate the suspect, determine the type of weapons available, or if the structure is barricaded or booby trapped. Modern technology has developed audio and visual monitoring equipment that will enhance a team's capability.

Night vision goggles and image intensifier equipment are suggested for scouting and night operations. Hand held mobile video cameras that are remote controlled and sensitive to both visible and infrared light have been developed. The single optic image intensifier is adaptable to a 35 mm camera. The video system is also adaptable to a rifle scope.

Fiber optic and micro optic technology has been developed to allow observation through pin holes in walls, floors, and ceilings. One optic device is offset 15 degrees to allow the user to view the entire room by rotating the scope. An under door optic has been developed to fit under a one-quarter inch space. The entire room can be observed. A 90 degree adapter allows the device to look up the door to detect barricades and booby traps.

Covert installation can be accomplished on plaster board walls by wetting the plasterboard with a mixture of vinegar and water and cutting out a piece at an angle to ensure that it doesn't fall through the space between the walls and possibly alert the suspect. A small hole is then made and the device is put into place. Hotel and motel rooms usually are constructed with common electric outlets. The operator can remove the outlet plate on the wall of an adjoining room and install the equipment.

Hard wire microphones and transmitters can be installed in the same way. During the Branch Davidian siege at Waco, Texas the FBI secreted transmitters in the insulation of boxes containing milk cartons sent in for the children. "Shotgun" and parabolic microphones have been utilized to monitor suspects. Wire taps, scanners, and equipment that monitors cellular telephones are effective. Cellular telephones emit an electronic serial number (ESN) that is particular to that specific device. Two types of ESN readers have been developed called "trigger fish" and "swamp box". Even though a cellular telephone does not have a hard line, the person still has an expectation of privacy, therefore, a court order is necessary.

Two United States government agencies employed swamp box technology during a hostage rescue operation in a foreign country. Two U.S. citizens were kidnaped in the United States and held in a foreign country as collateral for 200 kilograms of cocaine that a trafficker had been advanced by the cartel and had not paid for. The cartel members threatened to kill the hostages if remuneration was not forthcoming. Arrangements were made to "flash" the money at a neutral location under sniper observation and with a reaction team. The traffickers then made a cellular telephone call to the main trafficker to advise that they had seen the ransom. The "swamp box" identified the ESN and allowed interception of the conversation and tracking of the cellular telephone. Surveillance was initiated on the cartel members and the cartel leader by U.S. agents and host country law enforcement agents.

Surveillance resulted in the identification of a location that was guarded by cartel members and their movement indicated that the hostages might be at that location. The cartel members were well armed with an extreme propensity for violence. The hostages had already been held in captivity for more than one month. One hostage was a 12 year-old girl. The host country counterparts were not trained to affect the type of hostage rescue operation that would have a good chance for success. Most of their operations resulted in casualties on both sides. The U.S. agents would have had to obtain "Direct Action" clearance, and this was not probable because of the relationship between the U.S. government and the foreign country.

Direct Action is a term for a classified operation that is approved by the Joint Chiefs of Staff and National Security Council. Military CT operations are under the command of the Joint Special Operations Command (JSOC) which coordinates operations involving DELTA, DEVGRP, Air Force, Marine, and a SPECOPS helicopter unit called Task Force-160. The President approves a document called a National Security Defense Directive. This directive usually entails "neutralization", "extraterritorial rendition", or retaliatory military strikes.

It was predicted that the decision of the USG chain of command would be made to officially request that the host country initiate a hostage rescue operation to assuage their sensitivities and that there would be casualties. The determination was made to negotiate directly with the leader of the cartel. Representatives of the U. S agencies and the foreign counterpart agency visited the cartel leader and advised him that they knew that he had ordered the kidnaping and that he had command and control of the operation. He was advised that there would be tremendous enforcement pressure on his organization if the hostages were not immediately released. The hostages were released, and returned safely to the United States.

CHAPTER 15

Entry and Search Techniques

One of the most important parts in raid planning is back planning. Back planning is determining where to position the operators in order for them to effectively execute their assignment. For example, the operator who is expected to go the farthest should be near the point. The breacher should be near the point. The Team Leader is usually in the middle. Stacking personnel in vehicles should take back planning into consideration. At the briefing, each operator should be advised what position he will take in the assault. Furthermore, they should be advised the seat they are to take in the vehicle/conveyance. This should be done on a load manifest.

The formal briefing and equipment check is conducted at the Assembly Area. After a rehearsal, stacking vehicles is conducted. A rehearsal exiting the vehicles is recommended. The team then proceeds to a Rally Point which is an area that cannot be observed by the aggressors. The team then moves tactically to the Jump Off Point which is the last position of safety. The Team Leader notifies the Commander that they are at the Jump Off

Point. At this time the Commander notifies the sniper elements to switch from their frequency to the assault frequency. The Commander announces "I have control." Now the snipers have concluded the observation and intelligence phase and are an element of the assault. The Commander orders the team to proceed to the Set Point which is a location near the Breach Point where the team will make final approach to the Breach Point. The Team Leader advises they are at Set Point. The Commander orders them to proceed to Breach Point. The Team Leader stacks the assault team and they are ready to assault. He advises the Commander. The Commander orders the assault three times to avoid any breakdown in communications.

Movement technique for approaching a target building is dictated by several factors. Among these are the mission, cover and concealment, lighting conditions, type of breach, (single or multiple breachers), and terrain. In all cases, either a modified bounding or a bounding over watch technique will be used to approach the building. This will ensure that basic security is not violated and cover is provided the assault team. No two approaches will be alike as no two targets are exactly alike.

The assault team should, when possible, line up on the side of the door which provides them with the path of least resistance upon entering. The swinging door is an obstacle that is best avoided by lining up on the correct side. If the door swings inward, the team should line up on the hinge side. If the door swings outward, the team should line up on the doorknob side. Lining up on the correct side of the door will result in the fastest and smoothest entry possible.

Prior to entry, door position, individual equipment, and weapons positions are important. Assault team members should get as close to the breach point as possible, staying in a crouched position. They should never take their eyes off their respective areas of responsibility (especially the Point Man). Individual equipment should be kept to a minimum and configured so as to reduce noise and bulk, thus aiding in stealth and speed. Weapons will be held in the contact ready or low ready position pointed in a safe direction. the muzzle will not be pointed at another team member. Fingers will be outside the trigger guard.

If a covert approach from the Jump Off Point is possible, and security is maintained, the "thumb back" "squeeze up" technique will ensure all team members are lined up and prepared for entry. This reduces the risk of compromise by eliminating verbal or audible signals.

The Point Man assumes his position at Breach Point. His eyes and weapon are oriented on the door. When he feels comfortable with his position, he will signal the Back Up Man by passing back a thumb up with his non firing hand. The Back Up Man will acknowledge receipt by squeezing his thumb with his non firing hand. The Back Up Man will close in tight on the Point Man, with his weapon oriented in the direction he will move when he enters the building. If he is to clear left, his weapon will be on the left side of the Point Man. This ensures rapid target acquisition without sweeping the Point Man with his muzzle. After he has received the acknowledgment of the thumbs up of the Point Man he will pass the same signal to the man behind him. This man will take the same action. The only difference is that his weapon will be oriented to the opposite side, as he is going in the opposite direction upon entry. This procedure will be repeated down the line of the team. When the assault command is given, the last man in line will squeeze the man in front of him with his non firing hand on the shoulder. This will be repeated up the line. When the Point Man feels the squeeze, he immediately initiates the assault followed by the team.

Whichever foot the Point Man has forward, when set, should

be the same foot all other team members have forward. This will allow the team to make faster entry and minimize the chance of tripping over each other. It is recommended that the team position themselves approximately one foot from the wall to allow increased visibility upon entry. If a covert approach is not possible, the team will modify the thumb back, squeeze up technique to increase speed of entry.

A line-up (stacking), order of march, and areas of responsibility will vary according to the method of breaching to be used. A team SOP should be developed and rehearsed for these varying techniques to maintain a smooth, controlled, and secure approach, line-up, and entry. Another factor that may affect the approach and line up is the passing of danger areas such as windows. These actions should be rehearsed so that smooth and secure passage of these areas can be accomplished.

The first action taken by an assaulter is to clear the breach point. It is essential that all team members pass through the threshold of the doorway as quickly as possible. Failure to clear the doorway quickly can result in team casualties, because the doorway is the focal point of attention for anyone in the room. This has been identified as the "fatal funnel". By moving fast the team will reduce the chances of being hit by fire directed at the door.

The next action taken by the team is the elimination of the immediate threat. Team members should expect to encounter immediate threat targets, but not look for them. If an immediate threat exists, there will be no doubt in the mind of the operator that he has encountered one. Any hostile target that blocks the movement of an assaulter to his point of domination is an immediate threat. Not only is he a danger, but by blocking the assaulter's path he may prevent him from clearing his entire sector and thus may be a threat to the entire team and the mission. Key on the presence of weapons (pay particular attention to the hands) or violent action. Any individual putting the life of a hostage or operator in fear of grievous harm or death is to be fired upon until the threat is eliminated. Non aggressive acts will be dealt with using an active non-lethal countermeasure.

The next action to be taken is to clear the corners. It is essential that the corners are cleared immediately because these areas are often neglected, are usually occupied by team members as points of domination, if something is missed it leaves a potential threat behind the team, and these sectors do not have interlocking sectors of fire (double coverage). The number one and two men are initially responsible for the corners. If for whatever reason they are unable to accomplish this, the three and four men must pick up this critical area of responsibility.

Team members will move to their points of domination next. This movement is a smooth and deliberate movement with purpose. Domination of the room is critical. While in movement to their individual points of domination, the assaulters will collapse their sectors of fire, and upon arrival, maintain their weapons and attention oriented on their areas of responsibility. Their sectors of fire should be collapsed in such a way that all threat targets have been engaged prior to arrival at their points of domination.

Points of domination in a room are dictated by the location of the entry point in relation to the room itself. In the vast majority of rooms, doors can be grouped as either center doors or corner/ offset doors. With knowledge of the room configuration prior to entry, the team can preplan points of domination. If the room is unknown, the team must be able to determine the type of room they are in and correctly determine and occupy points of domination while clearing. This is not an easy task and can only effectively be accomplished through training.

The following is a procedure for a two-man deep penetration of a center door room: The Point Man will clear the "fatal funnel," engage any immediate threat, clear the corner to his front, shift his sector of fire down the long wall as he penetrates deep into the room. While moving long, his sector of fire collapses to within one yard off the muzzle of the number two man. Upon occupation of his point of domination, he maintains his weapon and attention in his sector. He must penetrate deep enough into the room to both clear his entire sector and effectively dominate the room. The second man will enter the room and clear in the opposite direction. His responsibility is to clear the corner to his front and collapse back to one yard off the muzzle of the Point Man while moving to his point of domination. His point of domination is the first corner he encounters. Occupation of these two opposing corners in the room serves to effectively dominate the room and provide angles of view that eliminates most possibilities of remaining dead space.

The procedure for a two man deep penetration of a corner door room is as follows: The Point Man enters, engages any immediate threat encountered, clears the corner to his front, collapses his sector while moving and occupies that corner as his point of domination. His final sector collapses to within one yard off the muzzle of the number two man. The second man enters, moves in the opposite direction of the number one man, engages any immediate threat encountered, clears his corner and collapses his sector while moving to within one yard off the muzzle of the Point Man. His point of domination is the corner opposing that occupied by the Point Man.

In a four man deep penetration, the Point Man goes deep, and the second man goes to the opposing corner. They both collapse their fields of fire to within one yard from the other operator's muzzle. The third man enters and moves in the opposite direction of the second man. he goes to the same side as the number one man and collapses a sector of fire that begins slightly off-center opposite of the direction he intends to move. The center of the room is determined by the center of the wall opposing the entry point. While moving far enough to get out of the "fatal funnel", he collapses his sector of fire to within one yard off the muzzle of the Point Man. He also has the additional responsibility of covering any personnel between himself and the Point Man. The fourth man enters and moves opposite of the number three man. He moves to the same side as the second man, collapses a sector of fire that begins slightly off-center opposite the direction he intends to move. In doing so the number three and four men's sectors of fire overlap and no possibility exists of an area of the room uncovered in the initial clear. He occupies a point of domination just out of the "fatal funnel" just as the third man did. He also has the additional responsibility of covering any personnel between himself and the second man. This clearing action takes very little time and is very effective if properly executed. The occupation of opposing corners, collapsing sectors of fire and understood areas of responsibility ensure a quick and thorough operation.

It is recommended that the "contact cover" procedure be utilized where the arresting operator is covered by his partner. Another recommendation is that the operator who makes first contact maintain custody and/or stand by the wounded or deceased suspect. Handcuff all suspects, regardless of their condition.

The "first in - first out" rule is suggested. The Point Man announces that the room is clear by loudly verbalizing his last name followed by "clear" and his last name followed by "coming out". This notifies other team members that the room is "clear" and that the entry team is coming out. The Point Man leads the team out. Many teams use a visual signal as well, such as, a "thumbs up" or flashing the light from their weapon on the floor outside the room to identify themselves to other team members.

Many times the exact configuration of the structure cannot be determined. Sometimes the Point Man will engage an aggressor and move in the opposite direction that was planned. No matter what direction the Point Man proceeds, the Back Up Man will assault in the opposite direction. This will dictate the direction additional assaulters will take depending on the size of the entry team. However, clearing corners, running walls, points of domination and sectors of fire must all be addressed.

One tactic called the "Snake" was developed to adapt to configurations that were not easy to scout and plan for. The principal is for each team member to "key off" the direction of the operator in front of him.

Another tactic is called the "running team" which was developed to search ships and multi-room structures such as apartment buildings, hotels, and motels. After initial entry, the Point Man will assess the situation and call up the number of operators to search the next room or rooms. He will verbalize "two up" or "four up" or as many operators as necessary for the next phase of the search. The Team Leader called the "hall boss" in this tactic coordinates the team movement and has "designated shooters" with him. If hostile contact is made, and "hot two" or "hot four" is verbalized depending upon the size of the room where the hostile contact is occurring, the "hall boss" reacts with the "designated shooters".

The "dynamic assault" tactic was developed for hostage rescue and incorporates the tactics discussed previously with an emphasis on speed, surprise, and diversion. This tactic requires rehearsal and highly skilled personnel. Dynamic assault has inherent danger in that operators can pass potential danger areas for the sake of speed and in the effort to rescue the hostages and neutralize the aggressors. Many narcotic enforcement teams utilize this tactic to prevent the destruction of drug evidence.

Most SWAT teams have a policy that discourages this tactic for the sole purpose of seizing evidence. There must be a life threatening factor to warrant a dynamic assault.

The "breach and delay" tactic was developed to react to situations where it is not necessary to dynamically assault the entire structure. A forced entry is made, followed by a delay, then entry is made. A modification is to make an initial dynamic entry, and then slow down the pace for a safer more methodical search. This allows the team to use mirrors, shields, and covert visual monitoring equipment.

A tactic to clear from the outside called "break and rake" was developed for a three man team deployed at a window. One operator uses an entry tool called a "pick" to break the window and rake the glass around all four edges. Curtains and blinds can be hooked and pulled out to clear the field of view and/or fire. The second man provides cover most often with an SMG. The third man deploys an NFD if the OPLAN requires. A fire extinguisher can also be used as a diversion. Break and rake teams are deployed in an "L" shaped configuration to provide safe sectors of fire.

When searching for suspects, look for furniture that has been moved, debris on the floor, footprints on the floor, walls, and carpet. Check all crawl spaces and attics. Look for dust prints that may have been disrupted when the suspect entered the crawl space or attic. Additional places to search are inside refrigerators, cabinets, under sinks, under box springs and mattresses, under piles of clothing, inside the trunk of a vehicle, and inside utility access panels. The search should be made with no assumptions being made as to a possible place of concealment.

When a suspect is contacted, verbalize the location to alert the rest of the team. Allow team members time to get good cover positions. Call the suspect out with hands in the air and fingers spread. Order the suspect to back toward your voice. Place the suspect in a proper arrest and control position. One procedure is to prone him out using the "contact cover" method. Handcuff the suspect, then search him.

Hallways can be cleared with a mirror before entering. The Point Man should stay low to allow team members to cover. Keep the area in front of the team lighter than the area you come from. Cover operators should use cleared rooms as cover. Move slowly enough to allow safe movement and good cover tactics.

Mirrors and shields are useful for clearing stairwells. Always have someone covering ahead of the person clearing. Light the area in front of the team. Most teams take the outer wall clearing up and down to provide the best visibility.

Covert entries are useful when a suspect is asleep or under the influence of alcohol or sedating drugs. Covert entries in a barricaded situation should be used, as a general rule, as a last resort. Many times a warrant service is changed when there is an exchange of gunfire and the suspect barricades himself in the building. Speed is not a factor and sound discipline is helpful, but usually the suspect is aware of the team's presence. Proper weapons deployment and the use of mirrors and shields are essential. Make sure all necessary equipment is inside the building and available. Stage the entry point to dominate as much of the interior as possible. Hand signals are the best way of communication. Consider returning to a safe room to discuss the next move with the team leader. Sit and listen for 10 to 15 minutes for movement. Avoid being backlit. Use a light as an advantage. Turn lights on when entering a room. Turn lights off when the room is clear. Follow the "one plus" rule. Expect a weapon. If the suspect is known to have one weapon, assume that there is another person with a weapon present. It is critical that the team leader control the movement of the team and pay particular attention to the positioning of weapons. A good rule of thumb is that if two weapons are pointing at the same location, there is probably a location that is not covered. Keep the team together and check all danger areas before continuing.

DYNAMIC ENTRY OPERATIONS

The following information was derived from an article written by Monte le Gould, California Department of Corrections, and Gary Rovarino LA Sheriff's Department Special Enforcement Bureau (Ret), and Owner of Tactics International regarding dynamic entry operations. For the purpose of the article the mission of dynamic clearing is to accomplish the following:

1. Execute a high risk warrant

2. Enter and clear a stronghold location for the purpose of hostage rescue

Dynamic entry is defined as a vigorously active, fluid, movement to dominate a location quickly without hesitation once the breach has been made. The following is a list of universal safety precautions:

1. Never move faster than you can accurately shoot and think.

2. Clear in a logical sequence to control the site through the use of trailors.

3. A minimum of two operators (1 cell) clears rooms.

4. Think at all times during the operation. Situational awareness is the key to recognizing threats and surviving.

5. Keep your finger off the trigger until you have a target to shoot at and are looking at the front sight on a lethal threat.

6. Never pass an area that has not been cleared.

7. Never turn your back on anything you have not cleared.

8. Stay away from corners and maximize distance to potential threat areas. Depth and distance equals safety.

9. Move correctly. Apply proper movement techniques so you have the ability to fire your weapon accurately immediately.

10. Use the front sight for accurate surgical shooting.

The basic team configuration is as follows:

1. Team Leader – responsible for planning and overview of operation and personnel

2. Scout or Pointman – Most senior and experienced tactical operator

3. Back up Man – second most experienced operator – back up to Scout or Pointman

4. Operator 4 – clears rooms, works with Team Leader

5. Operator 5 – clears rooms, works with Operator Six

6. Operator 6 – assists team where directed and fill in as needed

7. Trailor 7 – assists team where needed

8. Trailor 8 – assists team where needed

The four basic types of room clearing are:

1. Button Hook – Operators are staged on the door, step into the threshold of the doorway, reverse direction into the room rapidly clearing the entry point, moving continuously to a point of domination in the room. This tech-

nique is recommended for large doorways, garages, and warehouse doors. It allows the operator to enter from staged position and provides a method of clearing the 90 degree angle to the first operator's back as he enters. Operators have a tendency to drop their head and weapon momentarily upon entry into the room. In addition, the footwork is a little more difficult and not as smooth as the criss cross to maintain gunmount.

2. Criss Cross – Operators are staged on the doorway. They are on gunmount and move directly across the doorway threshold into the room rapidly clearing the breach point. This method is used for all standard doorways, interior or exterior. This may or may not be used on large doorways as described under the buttonhook. It allows the operator to maintain his footing and direction of travel while maintaining a solid gunmount. This is the preferred method when both operators can stage on the door and both can criss cross in a high low fashion. The first operator enters in a low crouch under the muzzle of the number two operator. Operators must remember to keep moving through the doorway and go through and out of the "fatal funnel".

3. Combination – first man button hooks and the second man leans over the first while moving into the room criss crossing into the room covering the opposite side. This method is recommended when the cell is stacked on a standard doorway.

4. "Slicing The Pie" or Limited Penetration – prepares the room for entry prior to the physical entry and allows visual clearing. Control can be maintained from the

exterior and 75-80% of the room can be cleared. Operators stack on the doorway; the first operator slices the doorway and stages. He and his teammate can now criss cross through the doorway.

ROOM CLEARING SEQUENCE

1. Clear the Breach Point

2. Move to Point of Domination

3. Initiate Verbiage to Control Threats

4. Engage Suspects

5. Search and Clear

6. Withdrawal

COMMON MISTAKES

1. Silhouetting the muzzle of the weapon into the threat room prior to entry

2. Failure of operators to enter room simultaneously

3. Failure to clear 90% angles

4. Failure to read off team mate's actions

5. Failure to communicate intentions or observations

6. Failure to remain calm

7. Failure to maintain gunmount and stance while moving

BUTTON HOOK ENTRY

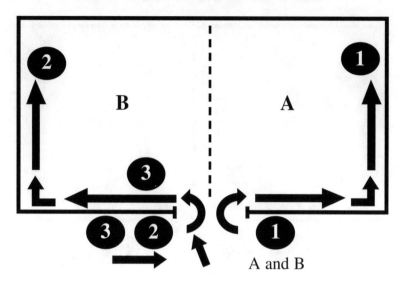

Staged Line Up   Zones of Responsibility

MODIFIED BUTTON HOOK

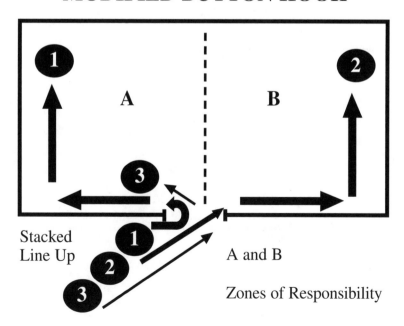

Stacked
Line Up

A and B

Zones of Responsibility

HIGH/LOW CRISS CROSS

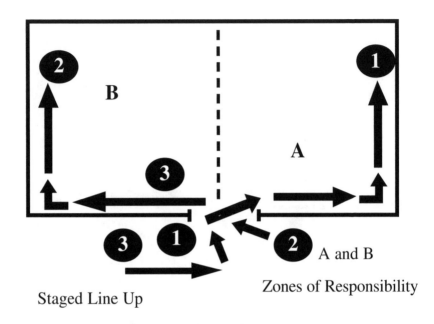

Staged Line Up

A and B

Zones of Responsibility

DYNAMIC ROOM ENTRY

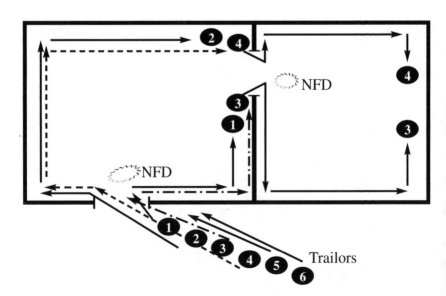

SLICING THE PIE

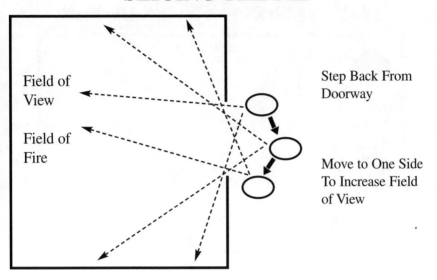

Step Back From
Doorway

Move to One Side
To Increase Field
of View

ISRAELI CLEAR

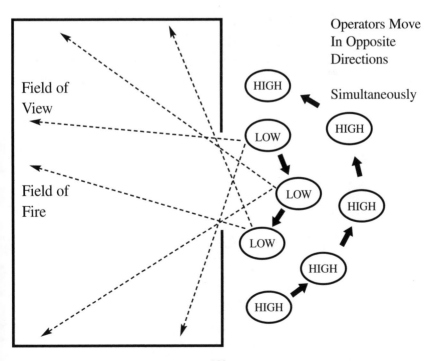

Operators Move
In Opposite
Directions

Simultaneously

CENTER DOOR LINE UP POINTS OF DOMINATION/SECTORS OF FIRE

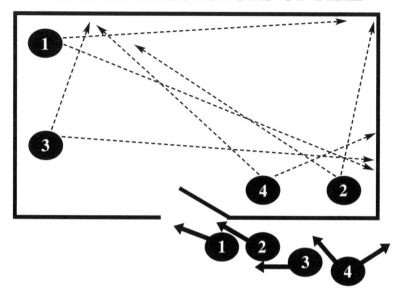

CORNER DOOR LINE UP POINTS OF DOMNATION/SECTORS OF FIRE

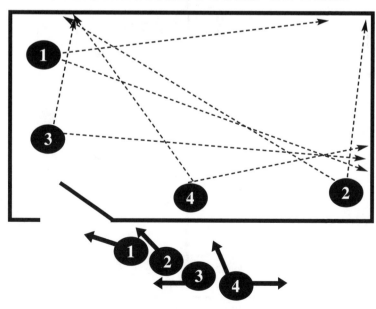

HRT – SECTORS OF FIRE

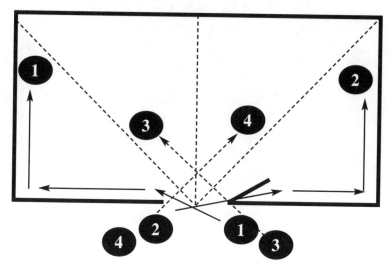

CRISS CROSS DYNAMIC ENTRY

2nd Story BMP

CHAPTER 16

Mobile Arrest/ Vehicle Assault

Most law enforcement officers will admit they have not always followed the basic principles for felony car stops and that some of the tactics they used were unsafe. Most of the tactics worked simply because the arrestee chose not to resist arrest and kill the officers on the day he was confronted. The application of good tactics combined with firearms proficiency, physical fitness, mental preparedness, and appropriate equipment will help you to survive encounters and not depend on "luck".

Vehicle stop techniques are continuously revised and improved upon in order to provide officers with new ideas and safer methods. They can be categorized as Compliant Vehicle Stops where the arresting officers remain at a distance behind cover and issue verbal commands to the arrestee. In the Non-Compliant Stop, the vehicle is boxed in and arresting officers rush the vehicle to arrest the suspect. This method is used often in drug enforcement. In an Emergency Stop, the suspect's moving vehicle is cut off by an arresting vehicle. There is a hazard of a severe collision in addition to the inherent dangers involved in conducting vehicle stops.

Good vehicle placement should include: Cover for the officers involved, Separation of the officers so they are not bunched in a line of fire from the suspect vehicle, and Surveillance of the problem area and all areas of response.

The single greatest tactical error when affecting a vehicle involved arrest is: failure to contain the suspect or suspect's vehicle. The second greatest tactical error is: engaging in a crossfire.

Pre-planned Stops occur when the officers have the option of selecting the time and place to make the stop and subsequent apprehension. For a preplanned stop the following factors should be considered:

1. Type of Vehicle

    a. Doors and type

    b. Interior design

    c. Lighting - interior and exterior

    d. Engine size, transmission, etc.

    e. Radio equipment, scanners, etc.

2. Subjects

    a. Number

    b. Descriptions

    c. Background (criminal history)

    d. A violence propensity

    e. Location of vehicle

3. Weapons

    a. Type

    b. Quantity

    c. Location

4. Undercovers and Informants

    a. Number

    b. Description

    c. Location in vehicle

5. Apprehension site

    a. Site affords concealment and cover for additional apprehension personnel

    b. Predetermined diversions

    c. Urban location

       (1) Types of streets, highways

       (2) Shopping centers, motel areas, parking lots

       (3) Speed and mobility of vehicle

    d. Rural area

       (1) Types of roads

       (2) Location of stores, buildings, trees, vegetation, fields

       (3) Speed and mobility of vehicle

6. Arrest team

    a. Number of officers available

    b. Number of vehicles

    c. Weapons and equipment

    d. Communications

Vehicle assault tactics require skilled operators, rehearsal, and a lag time of less than 15 seconds. It is best to assault the target vehicle from the rear on the same side as the suspect. Planning should consider the situation, urgency, hostage projected participation, suspect's background, number of assaulters and their assignments, hostage handlers, and type of diversion. Experience has shown that if a diversion is used, it should be instantaneous. During a 1.5 second fuse burn on a distraction device, a designated shooter will often be on his target and engaging before the NFD ignites. The third man in line hitting the fender with his hand to distract the suspect was found to be effective. Shotgun launched NFDs fired from the rear of the target vehicle over the top and toward the front were also found to be effective.

During the rehearsal phase, the location and target vehicle should be duplicated. The assault should be practiced from Jump Off Point to the rescue and hostage removal. Removal is accomplished by a designated assaulter calling to the hostage by name to come to him, and if the hostage "freezes" or fails to respond to verbal commands, he is physically removed from the vehicle away from the field of fire. The assaulters are armed with handguns to deliver head shots from close range from designated positions.

There are a number of ways to assault a vehicle. One tactic entails six shooters, three on each side, firing in a downward direction. Another entails two shooters and two backup men on the same side of the vehicle. Another tactic involves an "L" shaped configuration. Planning should take into account deflection from the windshield, shattering of side windows, "fogging" of rear windows, and the effects of spalling.

During the 1980s and early 1990s, United States Government enforcement agencies initiated a number of "proprietary operations" which were U. S. Attorney General approved undercover operations that entailed transferring the proceeds of drug cartel sales from the United States to foreign countries, primarily Colombia. This entailed "pickups" of bulk cash and the depositing of it into undercover bank accounts for subsequent wire transfer through offshore accounts to the recipient account in the foreign country. The average "pick up" was more than $200,000.00.

During the author's tour as DEA Assistant Special Agent in Charge in Los Angeles, he supervised hundreds of undercover transactions laundering more than $70 million for the cartels. Mobile and electronic surveillance was used extensively to protect undercover agents during pick ups. A "Compromised Agent Rescue" tactic was developed with the assistance of LAPD SWAT where a cover surveillance vehicle electronically monitored the transaction. This vehicle had two designated shooters and one rescue agent to extract the undercover agent. It was positioned to assault from the rear to allow the assaulters to be on target in less than 15 seconds. The three man team assaulted on the side of the suspect/hostage taker. The first man fired through the windshield downward for a head shot. The second man covered the rear seat. The third man would strike the rear fender of the target vehicle to distract the suspect and was responsible for going around in front of the vehicle calling the undercover agent to come to him and physically extract him from and away from the vehicle.

Tactical considerations should include the location of the undercover agent, location of suspect, rescue team members should wear soft body armor, approach on the suspect side, fields of fire are down, hostage moves out of the vehicle toward front, consider multiple suspects, rules of engagement, rescuers are armed with handguns and they must be in close proximity with "eyes on" the target vehicle.

Prevention is most desirable and this tactic is a last option when the undercover agent's life is in danger. The possibility of the use of deadly force is extremely high in view of the fact that the hostage taker most probably has a weapon pointed at the agent. Rapid deployment, dynamic assault, and surprise are essential.

VEHICLE ASSAULT
AREAS OF RESPONSIBILITY

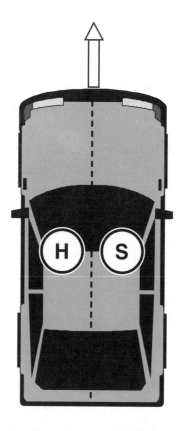

SIDE ONE   **SIDE TWO**

HOSTAGE   SUSPECT

CHAPTER 17

Linear Assault

Linear assault tactics, also called "tubular assault", were developed for hostage rescue operations on large conveyances such as commercial aircraft, buses, and trains. Incidents involving mass transit systems are caused by criminals, the mentally deranged, and terrorists.

In the United States, the most often utilized tactic is employed in situations that involve bus assaults. The operation is either a hostage situation or a barricaded gunman. It is emphasized that no hostage situation is static. It is always changing and planning is continuous.

Immediate deployment should entail the "CLEAR Approach": Containment, Long Rifle, and React (Emergency Entry). The five phases of a hostage rescue are:

1. Planning
2. Rehearsal
3. Movement
4. Assault
5. Withdrawal

There are four elements required for successful intervention:

1. Exact layout of target must be known

2. Entry team must be in position to strike within 10 seconds of the order from SWAT Commander

3. There must be sufficient personnel to dominate all areas of the threat location

4. The entry team must be able to protect the hostages within 60 seconds after intervention is discovered.

The operational philosophy is to surprise and overwhelm the suspects before they can harm hostages. Intervention is rapid, precise, and devastating. Once it starts, it continues non-stop until the hostages are secured.

The concepts of surprise, aggression, speed, and diversion are followed. The four basic objectives are:

1. Quickly take control of the area and dominate it.

2. Deliver accurate weapons fire if necessary.

3. Assure your sector of fire does not endanger another element of the entry team.

4. Complete your assignment without hindering your fellow team members from completing theirs.

Hostage rescue assault force personnel are broken down into three elements:

1. Ladder Teams

2. Breaching Team

3. Entry Team

Personal equipment is kept to an absolute minimum. Eye protection, Nomex gloves, and balaclavas should be worn by all members. The entry team will probably prefer to wear soft body armor and not wear ballistic helmets. Helmets should be worn by the Ladder Teams and Breacher Team.

Mission specific equipment such as distraction devices, mechanical breaching tools, and suspect/hostage control equipment are issued to specified personnel.

There is some general information that should be considered when planning a bus assault.

The five position door activating lever is adjacent to the driver. Full forward or rear activates both front and rear doors when the Master Switch is "On". With the Master Switch "Off", it opens only the front door. Front doors are air activated with approximately 60 pounds psi when closed. They can be manually defeated by pulling the doors apart. Rear doors lock automatically via a metal latch mechanism. The latch can be released via an electronic solenoid when the door handle is released and the Master Switch is "On". The brake system on almost all buses automatically locks when the air pressure in the lines falls below 55 pounds psi. An excellent way to disable a bus is to cut both lines to a rear wheel.

The type of glass is either safety, or plexiglass. Darker tint is usually plexiglass. Plexiglass usually will break if hit with a solid object, but some cannot be broken. Safety glass will shatter, but stay intact like a car windshield, and requires repeated strikes with a solid object to "gun port" effectively. There is minimal deflection by both types of glass of 9mm ammunition fired from a pistol or SMG.

The driver's window is safety glass with no locking mechanism. The air pressure release switch is always adjacent to the driver and releases pressure on the front doors only.

Some buses can be disabled by a toggle switch in the engine compartment. Other buses have a master switch in the battery compartment that will turn off all systems. All bus windows serve as emergency exits. Some models have additional emergency hatches on the roof. It may be possible to open them from the outside for limited penetration.

Detailed scouting, planning, and rehearsal are essential. Negotiators may be directed to use a verbal ruse to get the hostage taker(s) in a position where a long rifleman can take a shot. A casualty producing "diversion" from the long rifleman can precede a sniper initiated assault.

Ladder teams consist of a minimum of three operators. One carries the ladder which is padded on one end to reduce noise when placed up against the conveyance. The bottom should have a sharp point or edge to dig into the surface. The Ladder Man holds the ladder firmly from beneath the ladder with his back to the bus.

The Designated Shooter is usually armed with a handgun, but SMG's with collapsed stocks and machine pistols are also used. Remember that accurate fire is essential.

The third man's responsibility is to control the shooter and pull him down from engaging aggressors upon command from the Team Leader. Commands are usually by whistle. It is best to deploy an NFD under the conveyance or to the side opposite of the assault. It has been found that deployment inside causes smoke that inhibits target acquisition. The ventilation system does not clear the smoke from the conveyance fast enough. The number of ladder teams depends upon the configuration of the bus and number of suspects.

The Breacher Team consists of three operators. One man is responsible for opening the window on the driver's side of the bus and activating the door lever "Master Switch" and air pressure release switch if necessary. The second man covers the first breacher. The third breacher manually opens the front door.

The Entry Team consists of a minimum of five assaulters.

The two "High Cover" men occupy the extreme outer corners near the front and direct their attention down their sectors of fire according to their respective assignments. The two "Aisle" assaulters proceed down the aisle and clear each seat moving towards the rear. The Team Leader verbalizes commands to the occupants and controls the movement of the team. The operation continues until all hostages are evacuated and the suspects neutralized. The Team Leader may require additional personnel which can come from the Ladder Team or the perimeter.

The above tactic is for an assault on a static location. However, there are incidents when a bus is mobile and an ambush is the best option. Factors that immediately must be considered are the skill and stability of the driver, containment of the ambush site, destination of the bus, and communications with the driver.

Good locations for an ambush are bends in the road, brow of a hill, and construction areas that slow down and channel vehicular traffic. Distraction devices assist in the element of surprise, but should be deployed outside for the above cited reason.

Snipers should be deployed to relay information to the assault team and take a shot if the situation warrants. The possibility of injuries to passengers by a sudden stop should be taken into consideration.

Although rehearsal is preferred, it may be necessary to react to an emergency situation. Generally, buses do not vary much from each other. Seating is usually in pairs facing the front with a center aisle. An "L" shaped ambush with an assault from the front is the best option.

Trains present a different type of problem to assault in that they entail numbers of cars into which the suspect(s) can spread out into undetected. There are three basic types: Passenger, Freight, and Commuter.

Passenger trains are usually very long, pulled by more than one engine, and have a caboose for rail officials. The passenger cars are high from the ground with low glass windows that open partially. Each car has folding stairs on both sides at each end. There are bathrooms, restaurants, and some double deck cars with large windows for viewing scenery.

Freight trains are usually pulled by more than one engine. There are numerous types of cars and the train can be very long. There is usually a caboose.

Commuter trains are usually electrically operated. The cars are designed for seated and standing passengers. The internal layout is one large compartment with few, if any, partitions. The cars are relatively low and the windows are low. Most windows do not open. The double pincer type doors operate like those in buses. Access is possible from one car to the other. Construction is the thinnest of the three types.

Trains can be assaulted by ladder, vehicle, or helicopter depending on location and terrain. The status of control and operability of the engines is a main factor. Location of the train, suspects, and hostages is critical. Knowledge of the type and condition of the doors, avenue of approach, and blind spots is essential. Although an "L" shaped ambush could be used, such as an assault on a bus, it might be necessary to assault through maximum entry points, using a diversion, which provide immediate coverage and maximum fields of fire. As in all assaults, rehearsal is essential.

Another factor that is different from buses, is the number of hostages that must be evacuated to a reception area with medical service attending. EOD and fire fighting equipment should be on stand by.

The most difficult conveyances to assault are aircraft because of the large number of passengers, configuration, and height from the ground. Visibility is restricted through small passenger and cockpit windows. Hostage situations are seldom criminal acts, but the result of deranged persons or terrorists with demands usually to free incarcerated fellow terrorists. Terrorists are extremely difficult to negotiate with because of their motivation and accessibility to firearms, explosives, and training. Many are state sponsored and receive training and logistics from Lybia, Syria, Iraq, Iran, Yemen, Algeria, and Cuba. During the "Cold War", many terrorists attended Patrice Lumumba University in Moscow where they received indoctrination and training from the KGB. Ilyich Ramirez Sanchez (a.k.a. "The Jackal") is an alumni. Numerous incidents have documented terrorists' willingness to follow through on threats of execution of hostages and destruction of aircraft.

Aircraft can be broken down into two types:

1. Wide Body - aircraft is compartmentalized with three rows of seats and two aisles (i.e. 747, 767, DC-10, and Air Bus)

2. Narrow Body - that has a large single passenger compartment with two rows of seats with a central aisle

Doors and exit points are obvious priority considerations from both an assault and hostage evacuation standpoint. There are a number of general types that are unique to each aircraft:

1. Doors that are side-hinged and swing out (747,DC-10)

2. Doors with stairs hinged on bottom (commuter flights)

3. Doors that are electrically operated and hoisted upwards (767)

4. Door and stair combination that allow exit from tail area (MD-88, 727)

5. Emergency exits over wings (doors and windows)

6. Front door/step combination hinged on bottom

7. Cockpit emergency exit for flight crew

8. Hatches, cargo doors, and inspection doors that allow entry by maintenance and inspections crews

Information needed to give the assault team adequate intelligence include:

1. AIRCRAFT

Type and size

Location in airport

Approaches/ blind spots

Doors and hatches

Size and location of cordoned area

Utilization of support and emergency services

Airline personnel/expert advice and assistance on the aircraft

Sniper/ observer position for immediate viewing

Negotiations - Verbal, radio, or telephone

2. SUSPECTS

Number

Weapons and explosives

History, modus operandi

Attitude, confidence level

Demands

Negotiation effects

3. HOSTAGES

Number

Medical condition

Gender

Religion

Nationality

4. CREW

Number

Check the passenger list for any special passenger (i.e., sky marshals, military personal, law enforcement). These must be identified prior to assault by photo and seat assignment in case they decide to participate in the assault.

Crew's experience in hijacking drills

5. EMERGENCY SERVICES

EOD

Medical

Fire department

It is stressed that the scope of the operation is impressive. For example, a wide bodied aircraft would require 40 operators on the entry team using mass saturation of all entry points. The ladder teams, drivers, sniper/ observer teams, medical, perimeter, and security personnel, plus hostage reception units would necessitate more that 100 team members. A large number of ambulances would have to be on stand by as well as hospital trauma units.

Post assault responsibility relies heavily on existing airport units and supporting local law enforcement teams. These responsibilities include:

1. Hostage cordon area

2. Hostage reception team

3. Hostage evacuation

4. Assist with hostage debrief

5. Transport for arrested suspects

6. EOD and fire departments

7. Perimeter control of aircraft and operational area

BUS ASSAULT-INITIAL DEPLOYMENT

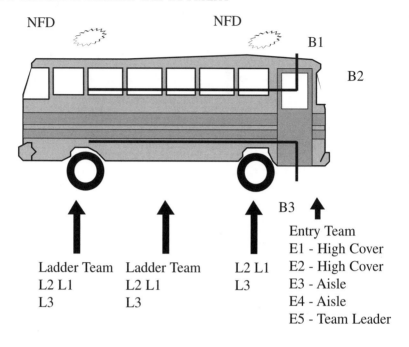

NFD   NFD   B1

                                                    B2

                                            B3

Ladder Team   Ladder Team   L2 L1   Entry Team
L2 L1   L2 L1   L3   E1 - High Cover
L3   L3   E2 - High Cover
                                        E3 - Aisle
                                        E4 - Aisle
                                        E5 - Team Leader

BUS ASSAULT-ON BOARD DEPLOYMENT

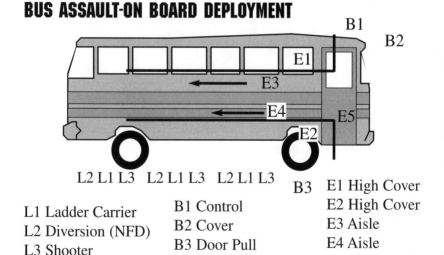

                                            B1
                                              B2

                                    E1
                            E3
                        E4   E5
                              E2

L2 L1 L3   L2 L1 L3   L2 L1 L3   B3   E1 High Cover
                                        E2 High Cover
L1 Ladder Carrier   B1 Control   E3 Aisle
L2 Diversion (NFD)   B2 Cover   E4 Aisle
L3 Shooter   B3 Door Pull   E5 Team Leader

160

Bus Assault Using Diversion

Train Assault Ladder Team

Train Assault Ladder Team

Train Assault Dynamic Entry

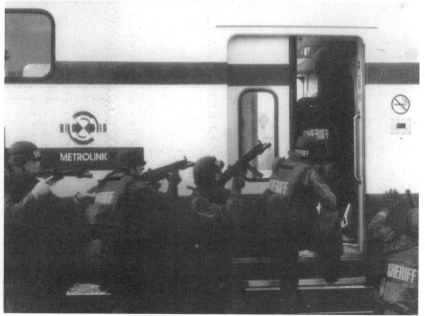

Train Assault Dynamic Entry

Train Assault Bang Pole Two NFD's

Train Assault Bang Pole Two NFD's

AIRCRAFT HOSTAGE RESCUE

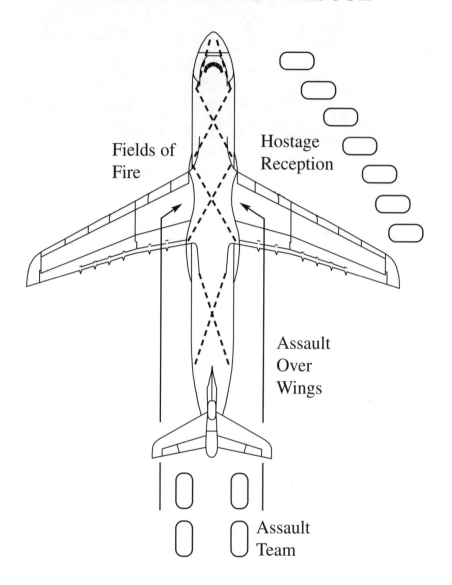

Fields of
Fire

Hostage
Reception

Assault
Over
Wings

Assault
Team

Ambulances

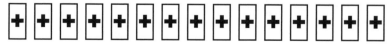

165

CHAPTER 18

Helicopter Insertion
and Extraction

The origin of current helicopter assault tactics can be traced back to French counter-insurgency operations in Algeria. The French then continued development in Vietnam which was the basis for later U.S. helicopter tactics in the Vietnam War. The tactic called "Eagle Strike" was developed using UH-1 helicopters to transport troops to the combat zone to immediately engage the enemy and prevent his escape. These aircraft were unarmed and were called "Slicks". "Guns" were UH-1 gunships armed with .30 and .50 caliber machine guns and rocket launchers to provide air support and suppressive fire on the landing zone. MEDEVAC helicopters ("Dust Offs") were also part of the assault force. Subsequently the AH-1 "Cobra" gun ship was added to increase air support with additional speed and firepower.

The concepts of speed and use of cover to avoid anti-aircraft fire were essential. There are three basic types of flying techniques for insertion:

1. Low Level Flying is used when out of range, but not so low that you have to climb to pass above trees and other ground obstacles.

2. Contour Flying entails flying so low that you have to climb over terrain features, but maintain a straight path.

3. Nap of the Earth (NOE) is the safest, but slowest method, in which you fly the helicopter at a very low level and fly around terrain features and obstacles rather than over them.

The central concept is to quickly insert a team without detection. It was determined that tactical teams needed the capability of responding to events that occurred in high rise buildings beyond the reach of fire ladders. This entailed deployment of snipers as well. Tactics involving the insertion of personnel onto rooftops utilizing small, turbine powered helicopters were developed.

Tactical personnel needed a field expedient or method of using a light observation, turbine-powered helicopter to transport up to four fully equipped officers (standing on the skids) onto rooftops or otherwise inaccessible areas without having to land or touch down. Using this procedure, personnel disembark the helicopter by stepping off the skids while the aircraft is at a low hover above the target.

Due to weight restrictions, single pilot operation is recommended regardless of the type of helicopter utilized (Bell Jet Ranger III or MD 500 Series). It is highly recommended the pilots be well-experienced aviators with some tactical knowledge as well as be mission oriented. Generally, the procedure requires the pilot (right side/Jet Ranger, left side/500 Series) to pick up one to four officers from a designated landing zone and deliver them to a target. The operators ride outside the aircraft, standing on the skids. Once at the desired site, the aircraft is brought to a hover approximately 12 inches to 18 inches above the surface. At that time, the "stick" or team leader, either via hand signal or radio, will direct all personnel to simultaneously step off the skids and deploy on the target. The aircraft then departs the area. With practice, "time-on-target" can be reduced to as little as five to 10 seconds for deployment of as many as four operators. This procedure can also be utilized to extract personnel from rooftops where time, officer safety, or the immediacy of the situation dictates expeditious evacuation from the area.

It is important to point out that during insertion operations, the helicopter remains at a hover, and generally does not touch down. During barricade situations, landing on a rooftop, or even touching a skid, can send vibrations throughout the building which in turn are easily detected by adversaries.

The following individual safety equipment is recommended:

1. NOMEX Utilities

2. NOMEX Gloves

3. Tactical Boots

4. Tactical utility belt with "D" ring

5. Four inch buck-style knife

6. Four 18 inch by one inch tubular nylon safety straps with quick release safety hooks

The above list does not include mission-oriented logistics such as weapons, soft body armor, radios, or other specific equipment.

The need to insert greater numbers of tactical personnel (more than four) would necessitate the use of larger types of aircraft such as the UH-1, UH-60, or CH-47. Fast roping and rappelling quickly places team members on the target site. Special

Purpose Infiltration/Exfiltration System (SPIES) are used to suspend teams. Harnesses similar to the kind used by parachutists, which attach to "D" rings, are stacked six feet apart and woven into a nylon rope. The downside of using larger aircraft is often availability, cost, rigging time, noise signature, and the inability to maneuver into confined spaces.

Smaller, turbine powered helicopters such as the McDonnell Douglas 500 Series or Bell 206B Jet Ranger III, offer a simple solution to personnel insertion requirements. Agencies that do not have helicopters can find them in the private sector or even news agencies. Liability issues become a factor when using private aircraft.

Preparation of the MD 500 includes removal of the rear doors. (The option of removing all four doors is entirely up to the pilot in command when visibility becomes an issue.) The purpose of this is two-fold: First, personnel riding on the skids, and standing between the struts, allow visual observation with all team members. Secondly, in the event of an aircraft emergency, personnel have the opportunity to relocate inside the aircraft. Removing the rear doors is easily accomplished and is consistent with sound safety practices. The MD 500 series have hard points in the area of the rear steps, which afford use of the 18" by 1" safety straps. These safety straps are utilized by all personnel standing on the skids. They are equipped with quick release locking hooks that can be fastened to the aft steps using 4 inch locking snap links. This procedure does not require any modification to the existing airframe, and merely requires a locking snap link with the desired number of safety straps attached to the rear step shaft prior to operations. The snap link slides on the shaft, affording movement of the safety strap. Operators equipped with tactical belts are able to secure themselves to the safety straps prior to aircraft departure.

The Bell 206B Jet Ranger III has high skid gear, but does not have the same hard points as the MD 500 series. Rear doors are removed. The only equipment required are quick disconnect door pins, safety straps, and individual tactical belts. Reconfiguring the aircraft takes only a few minutes. The safety advantages of allowing all operators to maintain eye contact with each other as well as provision to get inside the helicopter in the event of an emergency are the same as with the MD 500 series. "Pit-pins" can be pre-installed and removed quickly in the field. These pins are spring loaded, and with a simple push-twist-pull motion, can be removed without tools. The rear seats and backrests are removed to allow for additional space, if needed. Finally, the rear seat belts can be fastened together to provide handholds, and the required number of safety straps installed to designated hard points on both sides of the aircraft rear steps.

Weight limits, air density, altitude, aircraft performance, and fuel capacity all affect the amount of payload to be carried. When these factors are considered, personnel loads may have to be modified or reduced by one to two persons.

The insertion procedure varies according to the number of operators. The following procedures are for three and four man "sticks". Each stick will have a designated leader, and each member of the stick will have a designated number, ranging from one to four. The stick leader will always be identified as #1. On the 206B Jet Ranger team member positions include odd numbers being positioned on the right side of the aircraft and even numbers on the left. For control purposes, the #1 position will always be adjacent to the pilot. When designating members of a stick, consideration should be given to balancing heavier operators opposite each other for more even weight distribution.

When using the MD 500 series helicopter, the pilot will sit on the left side of the aircraft. Therefore, the numbering system will reverse. The #1 and #3 positions will be on the left side and the #2 and #4 positions on the right side of the helicopter.

Starting from the pick-up or pre-stage position (aircraft skids touching the ground), the #1 man, or stick leader, will position himself away from the front of the aircraft out of the rotor diameter and on the pilot's side. While maintaining eye contact with the pilot, the #1 man will await a nod from the pilot or radio contact instructing the entire stick to approach the aircraft. Once acknowledgment is received, the #1 and #3 men will approach the pilot side and #2 and #4 the opposite side. All men will move into their respective positions adjacent to the aircraft. These positions are approximately arm's reach plus six inches from the skid (allowing for lateral movement of the aircraft while at a hover). All men face inboard toward the helicopter and maintain eye contact with each other.

The #1 man raises his left hand, palm open, signaling the entire stick to approach the helicopter and secure a foot and handhold. As the #1 man slowly moves his left hand down, the entire stick will on-load the aircraft by stepping onto the skids. Since the aircraft skids are touching a hard surface, simultaneous on-loads are not as critical as it is during hover operations.

Each man hooks himself with safety straps, secures a handhold, and gives a thumbs up after visually inspecting each other. The #1 man, after ensuring each stick member is fastened in and receiving a thumbs up, will himself give a thumbs up with his right hand to the pilot to signify the stick is ready for departure. As the aircraft departs, operators adjust their positions toward the front of the aircraft and remain close to the airframe to reduce wind resistance and improve comfortableness. An important point to remember is that #1 and #2 stand to the rear of the front cross tube (Bell 206B) and #3 and #4 stand in front of the rear cross tube. The same positioning exists with the MD 500;

however, the cross tube is replaced by struts which connect the aircraft to the skids. Generally, handholds consist of #1 and #2 holding onto the roll bar of the front seat, while #3 and #4 hold the rear seat belts.

Upon approach to the designated target, the pilot will verbally give a "30 seconds out" warning to the #1 man signifying 30 seconds from the target. At this time, the #1 man will order either by radio or verbally to unhook from the safety straps. The hand signal to unhook consists of a clenched left fist alternating opening and closing quickly. The #1 man visually ensures all operators are prepared to disembark, and examines the landing zone to verify helicopter distance above the surface is 12 to 18 inches. Once the aircraft is stabilized, and acknowledgment received from the pilot, the #1 man will raise his left hand, palm open toward other stick members and with a slow movement downward, signal all operators to simultaneously step off the skids onto the landing zone.

During hover extraction operations, the stick is directed to on-load the aircraft, all operators should approach their designated stations slowly, secure a handhold, and lightly place a foot on the skid. When directed by the #1 man, they shift their weight onto the skid. When done smoothly, minimum movement of the helicopter will be noted. The key is not to jump onto the skid and remember not to attempt to push the helicopter out of the way while it is at a hover. Numerous rehearsals are highly recommended. When operating with less than four, the #1 position will always be on the pilot in command's side so as to maintain visual contact with him as well as other stick members.

The following is a recommended safety SOP:

1. Always approach/depart from the front of the helicopter and maintain eye contact with the Pilot.

2. Beware of the tail rotor, and never approach from the rear.

3. In the event of an aircraft failure, get inside and pull your feet up. Stay in until told to leave the aircraft by the pilot

4. Rally points are 12-3-9 on the clock

5. When approaching the aircraft on un level terrain, beware of the main blade height. On an extreme grade, move away from the low blade toward safety.

6. Always step together. Do not jump on or off the helicopter.

7. Upon loading, attach safety straps immediately and indicate thumbs up to stick leader.

8. Check and secure all loose equipment prior to loading.

9. Maintain weapons on safe. Point shoulder weapons down.

10. Step on the helicopter - foot closest to tail

11. Step off the helicopter - foot closest to nose

12. Don't deviate from the safety SOP

HELO OPS TEAM LOAD

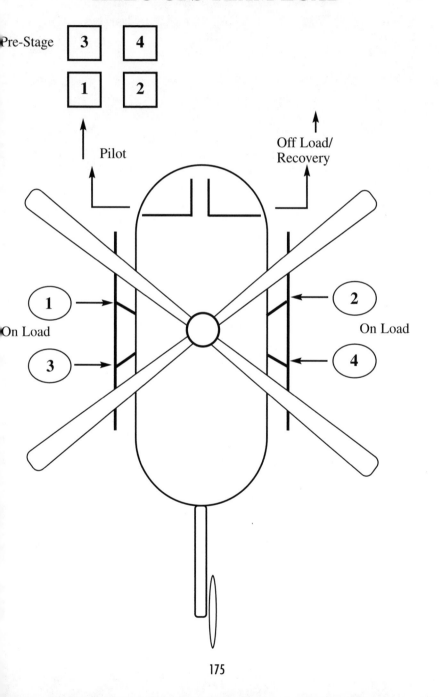

CHAPTER 19

Rappel and Fast Rope

Rappelling is defined as a descent from a precipitous point by means of a rope. It is an essential element in the list of skills for a tactical team. Rappelling is mostly used during operations involving high rise buildings, but is also used for helicopter insertion. It is inherently dangerous, and equipment should be routinely checked. Instruction should be by certified "Rappel Masters". Nylon line $\frac{7}{16}$ and $\frac{1}{2}$ inch in diameter 120 and 150 feet in length are most commonly used. The lines should be whipped to prevent unraveling. Wrap ends with vinyl tape sealing the end of the line with an open flame. Different lengths can be marked with colored tape for length designation: (1) blue, 50 feet, (2) green, 100 feet, (3) yellow, 120 feet, (4) orange, 150 feet, and (5) red, 200 feet.

Care must be taken to prevent equipment from deteriorating. Never step on or drag a rope on the ground, because dirt particles can cut strands. Keep rope dry and away from sharp edges such as rock, cement, or brick. Rope should be coiled when not in use. The outer sheath of the rope should be inspected for cuts, burns, and frays. If worn through, the rope is unserviceable.

If the outer sheath is serviceable, the inner core should be examined. This involves pinching the rope's entire length to feel for soft spots (Hour Glass) so as to identify internal damage to the core fibers, which should be monitored. As a guide, if the rope can be pinched more than one-third of it's original diameter, it is unserviceable. The pics of the rope should also be inspected. This is done by using a 10X magnifying glass. Look at the fiber bundles (pics). If more than 50% of the pics are broken, it is unserviceable.

The Running End of a rope is the free, or working end, of the rope. It is used to tie knots with. The Loop is a simple bend in the rope where the rope crosses itself. A Round Turn is a bend in the rope that runs around an object in such a manner as to complete a 360-degree turn with the pigtails ending up in the same direction. A Pigtail is the short end of the rope remaining at the end after tying a knot or coiling a rope. The Bight is a simple bend in the rope where the rope does not cross itself. The Standing End is the anchored end of the rope. A Half Hitch is a loop which runs around an object in such a manner as to bind onto itself.

There are four classifications of knots: Joining Knots, Anchor Knots, Middle of the Rope Knots, and Specialty Knots. A Square Knot is a Joining Knot that is used to tie the ends of two ropes of an equal diameter together. It maintains 43% to 47% of the rope's tensile strength. A Water Knot is a Joining Knot to tie two ends of tubular nylon. It maintains 60% to 70% of the tensile strength of the nylon. A Round Turn With a Bowline is an Anchor Knot used to tie a fixed loop in the end of the rope. It is used to anchor a rope to a natural anchor such as a tree. The knot maintains 70% to 75% of the rope's tensile strength. A Round Turn With Two Half Hitches is used to tie the end of a rope to an anchor. It must have constant tension to hold onto the anchor. This knot maintains 60% to 65% of the rope's tensile strength. The Bowline on a Bight is a Middle of the Rope Knot used to form two fixed loops in the middle of the rope. This knot maintains 70% to 75% of the rope's tensile strength. A Figure 8 Loop is a variation of the Overhand Loop and is easy to untie after it has held weight. This knot maintains 80% to 85% of the rope's tensile strength. A Directional Figure 8 Loop forms a single, fixed loop in the middle of the rope that lays back along the standing part of the rope. This knot maintains 80% to 85% of the rope's tensile strength. The Overhand Knot is a Specialty Knot that is used to temporarily whip the end of a rope. It maintains 60% to 65% of the rope's tensile strength. The Prusik Knot is used to put a moveable rope on a fixed rope of a different diameter. This knot maintains 70% to 75% of the rope's tensile strength. The Swiss Seat is a Specialty Knot made from a 12 foot sling rope used as an expedient harness for rappelling.

Protective gloves, usually leather with a wool insert, are essential to prevent severe rope burns. Another piece of equipment that is used effectively is the Descending Clog or Figure Eight. The rope is looped through the Figure Eight which is attached to the carabiner.

The "D" shaped carabiner (locking) is the most widely used carabiner due to safety of it being able to lock securely. Carabiners are used to attach ropes to anchors and personnel. Non-locking carabiners should not be used. There are five parts of the carabiner:

1. The Gate is the section of the carabiner that pivots open. This is the weakest part of the carabiner.

2. The Hinge Pin is the pin that the gate rotates on. It also holds the gate to the body of the carabiner.

3. The Locking Notch is located where the gate and body join the locking notch. This provides the means of closing the carabiner.

4. The Body is the solid steel shaft that makes up the carabiner, other than the gate. The strength of the carabiner is determined by the body structure.

5. The Locking Nut is only on the locking carabiner. It is a nut that will travel up and down the threads of the gate, locking the gate shut.

The Major Axis is considered to be the axis running perpendicular to the body of the carabiner from end to end. Any other load is considered to be loading the Minor Axis and should be avoided. The following areas should be checked on carabiners for serviceability:

1. The gate closes without sticking.

2. There is no excessive side-to-side movement of the gate. Excessive is considered to be ½" the body diameter.

3. The locking nut travels freely and locks securely.

4. There are no cracks or flaws in the metal. If a carabiner is dropped on a hard surface such as cement or steel, it should be discarded because of the possibility of a crack in the metal. Lightly oil carabiners to prevent rust from forming. Wipe all oil off prior to use. Ensure that there is not a build up of grime or dirt in the hinge area. If subject to salt water, rinsing in hot fresh water will remove the salt deposits.

Rappelling should be conducted under the instruction of a Rappel Master. During initial training, it is suggested to use two ropes for safety and to slow the descent. Equipment should be inspected before each descent. There should be a safety man called the "Belay Man." Verbalizations are given by the person descending: "On Rappel" and the Safety Man "On Belay". After the person has descended, he unhooks and announces: "Off Rappel". The rappeller should keep his legs parallel to the ground, or perpendicular to objects being descended, and walk downward. This can also be done facing downward (Australian Rappel). The rappeller repeatedly pushes off with his legs and controls the speed of the descent with his brake hand. Feet should be positioned below the waist to prevent inversion.

Free rappelling is conducted without touching a structure such as from a helicopter. It is important that the first step be far enough to clear the airframe and skids. Ballistic helmets are recommended for training in helicopter rappel to prevent head injuries and unconsciousness as a result of not clearing the skid.

Fast Roping was developed to insert teams even more rapidly than rappelling. Fast roping does not require hooking up to a line, and teams can deploy simultaneously. Larger aircraft are required, and the rope must be secured to the upper part of the helicopter to allow the operator to grasp the rope over his upper torso and hold it close to his chest. Some operators wrap their legs around the rope to slow descent. If operators rapidly descend in succession, it is important for all descending operators to clear the landing area or the assaulters will pile up on each other. This can reduce the advantage of the rapid insertion.

Rappel towers are not expensive or difficult to construct. It makes a good team project. Plans can be obtained from SWAT Teams and military units. Some towers have a helicopter body set up for rappel and fast rope at the top of the tower. Another design has a wall on one side and a helicopter skid on the other.

Some law enforcement managers feel rappelling training is

unnecessary. It is recommended that tactical teams have this capability in the event it is required. The training is also a confidence building experience. It is recommended that operators be trained in fast rope as well as rappelling techniques to enhance the team's deployment and helicopter insertion capability.

CHAPTER 20

Civil Disorder Countermeasures

When a municipality is confronted with a situation which may escalate into civil disorder, a law enforcement agency must establish control by reacting quickly to restore and maintain order, protect lives, protect vital facilities, arrest violators, and protect property. Specific missions may include:

1. Conventional crowd control

2. Patrol of hostile areas

3. Response to calls for service requiring multiple officers

4. Security for field personnel in hostile areas

5. Situations involving hostile crowds requiring chemical agents

6. High profile patrol operations

7. Life threatening events requiring immediate action

The appearance of an orderly, well organized, highly disciplined contingent of police officers will often cause a disorderly group to disrupt their activities. The Mobile Field Force (MFF) concept was developed to provide a fast effective method to assemble and deploy a platoon size tactical force of existing on duty personnel. It is adoptive to both spontaneous and pre-planned events. The MFF should be commanded by a Lieutenant with a Sergeant as Assistant MFF Commander. There are four Squads commanded by a Sergeant.

RECOMMENDED EQUIPMENT:

(13) Marked Vehicles
(1) Van
(19) Radios

An MFF Kit should include the following:
> Area Standing Plans - including command post sites
> Penal Code
> Vehicle Code
> Hazardous Materials Emergency Response Guide Book
> MFF Guide Book including emergency plan forms
> Short Form Arrest Book
> Release From Custody/Notice to Appear
> Plastic handcuffs
> Cutter for plastic handcuffs
> Marker for plastic handcuffs
> Flares
> Bullhorn
> First Aid Kit
> Fire Extinguisher
> Banner guard tape
> Bottles of white shoe polish - to mark vehicle assignments on windshields

Polaroid camera and film

Chemical agents

Chemical agent masks

Street Guides and Maps

Heavy duty plastic trash bags

Bolt cutter

37 mm less lethal munitions launcher and projectiles

Binoculars

Cellular phones

Video camera

Ammunition

Fragmentation vests

Ballistic helmets

BASIC FORMATIONS

Basic formations are adopted to the situation and are:

"In Trail" - the basic formation used when traveling from location to location. This formation can be used in squad or platoon strength and, if swift response is needed, with emergency lights and sirens activated.

"On Line" - begins from the "In Trail" formation and three vehicles in the squad proceed to a position parallel to each other. On command the driver of vehicle #2 moves to the left and parallel to vehicle #1. Simultaneously, the driver of vehicle #3 moves to the right and parallel to vehicle #1.

"On Line - Skirmish" - deploys MFF officers on foot supported by their vehicles.

"Bump" - begins from the On Line formation. Vehicles' emergency lights and sirens are activated during this action. This tactic is designed to have a psychological effect on a hostile crowd and move them out of an area. The purpose is not to intentionally strike pedestrians with vehicles. Vehicles alternatively move forward one half the vehicle length.

"Citizen Rescue" - using a squad size deployment begins with police vehicles In Trail with emergency lights on and sirens set at "wail". Vehicle #1 forces the crowd away and drives to a position in front of the victim and/or his vehicle. Vehicle #2 stops next to the victim. Vehicle #3 takes a covering position at the rear of the victim. The rear passenger officers in Vehicle #2 perform the actual rescue. After the victim is inside Vehicle #2, there are several options:

1. The victim and officers are removed in Vehicle #2

2. If the victim's vehicle is operable, an officer from Vehicle #2 can drive it out by falling In Line between Vehicles #2 and #3.

3. One officer from Vehicle #2 can fall back and move out with Vehicle #3.

No matter what option is selected, the driver of Vehicle #3 changes the siren to "yelp" to signal the squad leader that the plan is complete. Vehicle #1 then leads the others out of the area In Line.

"Convoy Stop" is a tactic which was developed for use when several suspect vehicles are to be stopped at the same time. This type of stop is one of the most dangerous situations. Probable cause must exist to make the stop. The element of surprise is essential. Well lit and back stopped locations with reduced chance of interference from pedestrians or passers-by must be identified for the execution of the stop. This tactic should not be used on more than five suspect vehicles. If more, two squads should be combined and work as a team.

The Convoy Stop is affected by the lead police vehicle stopping at an angle in front of the first suspect vehicle, the middle police vehicle should be positioned at the center of the convoy, and the last police vehicle is behind the last suspect vehicle. The maneuver is done simultaneously by all three police vehicles. All police officers exit and take positions of cover along the drivers' sides of the patrol cars. The driver of the middle patrol car directs the suspects via the P. A. system. The middle patrol car has the best visual contact with the suspects. This positioning avoids cross fires between officers. Preselected officers have rear security assignments.

To supplement the MFF a tactical team could be organized to form a Tactical Response Force (TRF) for SWAT and rescue assignments. One traditional role would be counter-sniper during civil disorder and to protect fire fighters. Equipment such a less lethal, .223 and .308 caliber rifles, NFDs, armored vehicles, and utility vehicles with running boards and "sun roofs" to post counter-snipers are recommended.

The TRF responds to high risk immediate action requests and to clear hostile areas. Many departments have developed elements to respond to these types of situations during civil disorders.

Departments should consider assistance from other tactical teams, the National Guard, Department of Defense, Federal Enforcement Agencies, and the Red Cross in situations that require additional manpower and support. A protocol should be worked out in advance at the command level to prevent friction resulting from different SOPs and jurisdictions. For example: In some states, federal agents do not have "peace officer" status and, therefore, could not enforce state statutes. They would have to be deputized as law enforcement officers of that state to legally assist the department. In some states federal agents can be deputized as U. S. Marshals which would give them the legal arrest powers of a county deputy sheriff. Some states grant law enforcement power to any civilian that is ordered or requested to assist a law enforcement officer. With previous planning and coordination, additional resources can be identified and brought on line if necessary and the liability issues can be addressed.

An example of inter-agency coordination is the cooperation that occurred in the 1992 civil disorder in Los Angeles. Many local law enforcement and federal agencies as well as the National Guard assisted LAPD. A great deal of equipment was loaned and brought on line from the Department of Defense, through federal agencies, to the LAPD.

Federal agencies assigned their tactical teams to assist the LAPD in protecting fire fighters from snipers. I was stationed in Los Angeles at the time as Assistant Special Agent in Charge of the DEA office, and the DEA team had the responsibility to protect the Roybal Federal Building which housed federal agencies and courts. DEA was then given the hostage rescue responsibility for that building. This allowed the LAPD Metropolitan Division and D Platoon (SWAT) to respond to more immediate problems and not have a contingency for the federal building. DEA Los Angeles sent an "UNODIR" (unless otherwise directed) teletype to DEA Headquarters in Washington D. C. stating that the DEA team was equipped, and trained for this assignment and, "Unless Otherwise Directed", would assist LAPD. The DEA team consisted of ex-Marines, U. S. Army Airborne, Special Forces, and Rangers, and U. S. Navy SEALs. Four of the team had previous SWAT experience. Two were Vietnam combat veterans. The team had received training from LAPD SWAT and LASD SEB and had developed personal relationships with both teams. The Los Angeles Office had the best trained and equipped team in DEA. DEA Headquarters would not officially sanction the team, because they were concerned other DEA offices and management could be liable if their training and equipment was substandard to what Los Angeles had developed. I was given tactical assignments with no official backing from Headquarters. There was no response to the "UNODIR" teletype, as usual, and the team was deployed. My boss stayed at home in the suburbs until after the riot was over and order had been restored to the city. I gave him daily SITREPS by telephone. In this way Headquarters and my boss were insulated and could always blame me if anything went wrong, and initiate an internal investigation on me for using "un-authorized" equipment. There were no problems. (SWAT -1, MARPLOTS -0)

MOBILE TACTICS
"IN TRAIL FORMATION"

Squad Size

12 Personnel
3 Vehicles

1 - Squad Leader
3 - Officers

4 - Officers

4 - Officers

<u>MOBILE TACTICS</u>
"ON LINE/SKIRMISH"

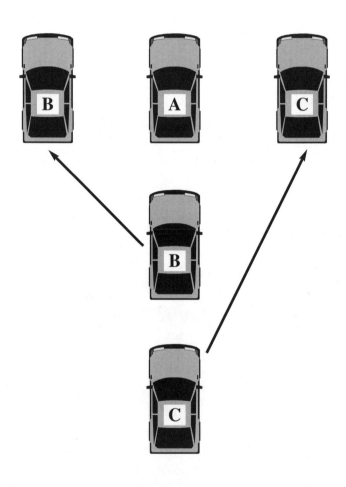

MOBILE TACTICS
"BUMP/SURGE"

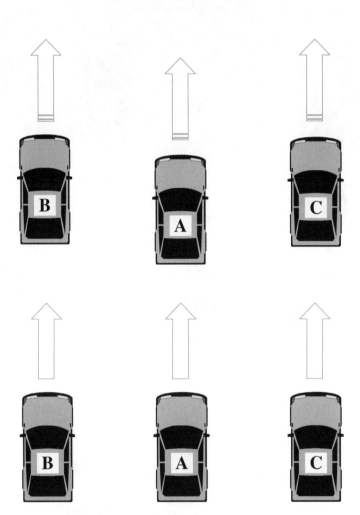

MOBILE TACTICS
"RESCUE FORMATION"

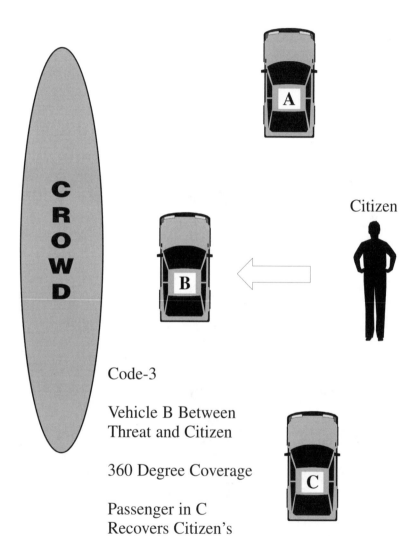

Code-3

Vehicle B Between
Threat and Citizen

360 Degree Coverage

Passenger in C
Recovers Citizen's
Vehicle

CHAPTER 21

Scouting

"Hoorah boys we've got em." (Colonel George Armstrong Custer, Little Big Horn, Montana Territory, June 25, 1876)

Scouting is an integral part of raid planning and execution. A good look is worth "a thousand words." But, being able to scout a location is a "learned technique." The operator will learn what clues he should observe and remember what dangers are evident and what techniques are available to assist in a successful scouting mission. Scouting will become "second nature" to the operator, as along as attention is paid to detail and the obvious.

To enable the operator to successfully plan, execute, and communicate to others the results of his scouting mission, a few techniques will simplify this process, and the operator will learn to be proficient as a scout. Training and practical exercises will reinforce the concepts of successful scouting techniques and procedure for the operator's future.

The following is a basic scouting format:

I. LOCATION

    A. Reference Points, Address

B. Bars - windows, doors

    1. How attached

    2. Backing Mesh

    3. Double locks

    4. Evidence of fortification

C. Evidence of children, elderly, disabled

    1. Bicycles, swings, crutches, wheelchairs, etc.

D. Access Points - Upper Floor

    1. Front, back doors.....Where is cover?

    2. Steps ....How many?

E. Photographs

    1. Drive by

    2. Aerial

II. FIELD OF VIEW - FIELD OF FIRE

A. Field of View

    1. The areas which can be observed but not completely covered by weapons fire.

B. Field of Fire

    1. The areas which can be covered by weapons fire and suspect engaged.

III. SCOUTING

A. Surveillance Capability for Intelligence

B. Floor Plan Sketch

C. Target (TGT) Site Numbering

    1. Number the target site clockwise

    2. Number openings left to right

    3. Number floors bottom to top

D. Look Outs

    1. Where, how many, signals

    2. Dogs

E. Friendlies in Area

    1. Approach routes

    2. Perimeter control

IV. Scouting Plan/Order (as appropriate)

The basic floor plan of a house can be determined by scouting. The types of draperies and curtains indicate the function of a room (i.e., living room, kitchen, bedroom). Chimneys will indicate fireplaces and stoves. The toilet can be located by the ventilation pipe on the roof. Furthermore, many bathrooms have smaller windows with frosted glass. The types of glass should be determined to brief sniper/observer teams to assist them in determining their deployment and project taking immediately incapacitating shots through glass if necessary.

TARGET SITE NUMBERING

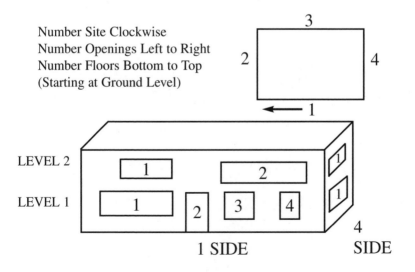

Number Site Clockwise
Number Openings Left to Right
Number Floors Bottom to Top
(Starting at Ground Level)

CHAPTER 22

Raid Planning

The purpose of a raid is to disarm the adversary and impose your will, arrest/perpetrator neutralization, and seize evidence. Tactics must be flexible to adapt to changes in situations. Tactical considerations include:

- Range
- Type and caliber of weapons
- Protective equipment
- Ladders
- Saw
- Ram
- Explosive breaching
- Rapelling equipment
- Ballistic shields
- Radios
- Hand signals
- Sniper/Spotter team
- Noise flash devices

- Diversion
- Less lethal munitions
- Break and Rake
- Aerial photography
- Vehicle stacking

Back planning is a good technique to determine the placement of operators in conveyances and determining their line up on the assault team. The operator that has the farthest to go is in the front of the line and occupies the lead conveyance. This technique results in simultaneous deployment of operators.

Raid Planning should consist of issuing a Warning Order to notify the team of the general mission statement. This is followed with an Operations Order (OPORD) which is a detailed written instruction for each team member which will specify his assignment. Load Manifests indicate specific assignments in conveyances as a result of back planning. A Warrant Service Information Sheet indicates the operator's assignment, equipment, and conveyance. The following are basic examples of a Warning Order, Operations Order, and Warrant Service Information Sheet, and Load Manifest:

WARNING ORDER

1. Situation
   a. Brief statement of type of action required - search/ arrest warrant execution

2. Mission
   The mission of the unit is to:
   a. time   b. place   c. date
   d. who   e. what   f. where

3. Execution

The mission will be accomplished by:

a. Unit

1. Assignment

4. Service/Support (Administrative)

The following equipment and support will be needed:

a. Uniform of the day

b. Weapons

c. Equipment

d. Chain of Command

1. Command Post

2. Operations Commander

3. Team Leaders

4. Communications

5. Special Instructions

a. Designated shooters

b. Less lethal munitions

c. NFDs

OPERATIONS ORDER

1. Situation

a. Adversary

b. Friendly

c. Civilians - hostages, homeowners, bldg. manager, etc.

d. Weather

Sunset

Moonlight

Cloud Cover

Illumination

Temperature

BMNT (Beginning Morning Nautical Twilight) - One half hour before sunrise a person sleeps the deepest.

e. Terrain

f. Location

2. Mission
   a. Type of action required
3. Execution
   a. Leader briefings
   b. Specific assignments
   c. Route/alternate route
   d. Action at objective
   e. Time of departure - Rally Point
   f. Order and method of movement
   g. Action on hostile contact while approaching Ambush - Action on compromise
   h. Coordination with other agencies
4. Support Element
   a. Hospital
   b. Police
   c. Public Works
   d. Fire Department
5. Command/ Communication
   a. Chain of Command
   b. Methods of Communication - radio, cellular, hand signals, SATCOM
   c. Command Post
   d. Time Set
   e. SIT REP - Situation Report
   f. Time and Place of Briefing/Debriefing
6. Special Orders
   a. Sniper/Observer
   b. Less Lethal Munitions
   c. NFDs

WARRANT SERVICE INFORMATION SHEET

ADDRESS:_____

_____

DESCRIPTION OF TARGET:

B/H - BULLHORN   H - HOOKS   B/R - BREAK and RAKE

E - ENTRY   D - DRIVER   T/C - TRAFFIC CONTROL

NFD - NOISE FLASH DEV.   V-VAN   F/E - FIRE EXTING.

C - COVER   B/C - BOLT CUTTER   L- LADDER

U - UNIFORM CONTAINMENT   G - GAS

LL - LESS LETHAL

ASSIGNMENTS

NAME	ASSIGNMENT	EQUIPMENT	VEHICLE
1._____	_____	_____	_____
2._____	_____	_____	_____
3._____	_____	_____	_____

LOAD MANIFEST

CHAPTER 23

Long Rifle Program

To put it succinctly, you cannot have a viable tactical team without long rifle capability. This includes both tactical long rifles with iron sights, or optics around four power, and long-range rifles with scopes usually ranging from three power to twelve power. Most teams' tactical rifles are .223 caliber semiautomatic rifles. Most long-range/sniper rifles are .308 caliber bolt action. Rifles provide accurate, effective fire at extended distances and are essential to protect the team as they approach the objective and react to immediate threats. Deployment at extended distances often places the rifleman out of the range of the adversary and provides a vantage point from which to pass real time intelligence on the adversary's movement to assist in raid planning.

A tactical long rifle should be accurate at no more than three minutes of angle (MOA). This is roughly 1½ inches at 50 yards, 3 inches at 100 yards, and 6 inches at 200 yards without making sight adjustments for elevation or windage. This accuracy standard translates to consistent head shots out to a distance at which most people can identify specific facial features (50 yards), and the capability to shoot body size targets in mid-torso at 200 yards, or farther, with consistency. Most law enforcement long rifle shots are taken at less than 100 yards.

Most snipers prefer a Remington 700 .308 caliber bolt action rifle with a 3 - 10X scope with a mil-dot reticle. Laser range finders are a preferred piece of equipment. A miscalculation of the range can result in missing the target. Accurate range cannot be calculated satisfactorily by visual estimation.

It is a consensus that a sniper should be a disciplined and patient individual. He must be very physically fit with good cardiovascular conditioning, eye sight, hand eye coordination, and motor skills. In the author's opinion there is no gray area in the matter of physical fitness. The physical demands of deploying and "hiding" are most often more rigorous than those experienced by the entry team. Snipers should be at the highest standard of physical fitness - especially cardiovascular. Psychologically, a sniper must be emotionally detached with focused attentiveness, and have the ability to depersonalize the adversary. Some teams remove the sniper from the scene after he has neutralized an adversary and do not allow him to see the results and effect of the bullet on the body. The theory is that the sniper remains detached from the incident. On the other hand, a great deal can be learned by personally observing and analyzing the results of the shot taken against the "dope" on the rifle and equating it to the range, angle, light condition, weather, and all the other factors that effect marksmanship and wound ballistics. There are always "lessons learned".

There is a consensus among snipers that there is not enough realistic training. This the result of a lack of training time for the team as a whole (usually one day per month), and a lack of understanding by the team commander of what training for snipers is required to maintain proficiency. One basic training program would include:

1. Weapons zero at different known ranges

2. Practice on targets at unknown ranges

3. Shooting moving targets

4. Night firing

5. Shooting in pairs

6. Command fire sequence

7. Shooting through glass barriers

8. Deployment in urban environment - "Urban Stalk"

9. Different weather conditions

Sniper/Observer Teams should practice with the entry team and rehearse scenarios of anticipated "call outs".

Deployment of Sniper/Observer Teams in an urban environment, "Urban Stalk", has been identified as a critical element in sniper training that is often overlooked by the team commander. Many commanders want to "take the high ground" and get a visual in a short period of time, sometimes even dictating the location where the sniper is to deploy. Joint training and candid debriefings should educate the commander to allow the precision riflemen the flexibility to deploy properly.

Snipers deploy to a location under the cover of the observer. The location is not always the highest point, and in fact, most situations require that the sniper be at the same level as the adversary or slightly higher. It has also been found that it is not beneficial to get too close to the target site and to depend on the optics and long range capability of the weapon for which they were designed. The technique of carrying weapons and equipment in cardboard boxes and dressing in civilian clothes has been a successful deployment practice for inserting into a nearby building. Roof deployment often silhouettes the team and necessitates building a "hide" most often out of a cardboard box.

Open windows of an adjacent building have proven to be excellent urban "hides". Snipers deploy back into the room to avoid detection, but not too far so that it limits field of fire. Burlap hung over the window and behind the sniper prevents detection. Duct tape has been used to simulate window panes. It was found that opening more than one window draws less attention to the "hide".

Snipers have developed "range cards" that divide the target site area into sectors. Then objects are selected as points of reference and ranges computed for coordination purposes. Sectors are identified by letter or number. The sniper/observer team can identify a suspect at a pre-determined range and pre-determined site. At the time of deployment, a "hasty range card" is made within 30 minutes to estimate ranges to probable threat areas. Then a "detailed" range card is made to include all essential information the team may require. This usually takes 60 to 90 minutes.

Range cards provide accurate range information to a number of positions. Threat Reference Points (TRP) are ballistic/visual reference points that have been identified. There are usually no more than two to three TRPs per sector. A SOP for range cards should be developed so that relief will be able to understand the data that has been recorded on the range card.

Another critical element that has been identified for additional training is shooting at moving targets. This is understandable because of the increased liability pressure on law enforcement in general and specialized teams such as SWAT in particular. Snipers cannot develop the confidence to take a life saving shot if they do not receive the commensurate training. It is true that moving targets are more difficult to hit than stationary targets, especially paper targets on the range at known distances on a clear day. The difficulty increases as distance and speed of movement increases. Now add low illumination and inclement weather. When is the last time you trained on a rainy night?

To shoot accurately at a moving target it is necessary to be able to get a proper sight picture on the target and then move the point of aim in front of or onto the front part of the target based upon the distance and speed of movement. This technique is called a "Lead". The following are general lead guidelines:

1. 100 - 200 yards
    Walking target at 90 degrees - front edge of target
    Running target at 90 degrees - lead by body width

2. Muzzle - 100 yards
    Walking target at 90 degrees - inside front edge of target
    Running target at 90 degrees - lead by ½ body width

3. Diagonally moving targets

Slow moving targets moving at diagonals toward or away from your position are a common occurrence. These confrontations usually occur at distances of a few feet to a few yards. If the target is moving at a very slow walk and the distance is within approximately 25 yards, aim just in front of the intended point of impact.

If the target has established a pattern of moving and then stopping momentarily, shoot when the target stops. No lead is necessary.

If the target has a hostage in close proximity and the hostage is in front of the target with the hostage's head or body partially covering the target, and the target is moving at a slow walk, aim just to the rear of the trailing edge of the hostages head or body.

Another factor that has been identified as being critical to accurate delivery of rifle fire is glass barrier penetration. It has been determined that muzzle - to-glass distances within five feet adversely deflect a bullet. Conversely if the muzzle- to-glass distance is extended and the projectile is ballistically superior to the glass, accuracy will not be affected. The closer the target is to the glass, the less deflection, and more probability of an accurate shot exists. Spalling, the cone shaped spray of glass particles, should be taken into consideration. The degree and extent of spalling depend on the type of glass and velocity of the bullet.

The criteria for making a glass penetrating shot are:

1. Will the bullet penetrate the glass?

2. Deflection

3. Bullet speed and mass after penetration

Factors to consider are:

1. Distance from rifle to glass barrier (drop)

2. Thickness, type, and angle of the glass barrier (penetration and deflection)

3. Distance from glass barrier to target (acceptable degree of deflection)

A bullet must remain intact enough to constitute a lethal projectile. When a high caliber round like the .308 passes through glass, there is always a degree of deflection. The sniper must be able to determine the acceptable angle of deflection in making the decision to take the shot or not. Experience has shown that shots taken by .308 caliber rifles through car windows have hit their target because of the close proximity to the windshield and minimal deflection. However, glass barrier tests, in general, have shown that results are unpredictable. Degrees of deflection vary from round to round and there is a great deal of deflection variation as the thickness of glass increases.

One technique to breach glass barriers is multiple simultaneous shots. This is one of the better options for thick glass. A great deal of practice is recommended.

Sniper training can be arranged through police departments and federal agencies and, in particular, the U. S. Army, U.S. Marines, and U.S. Navy SEALs all of whom have excellent sniper training programs.

In conclusion, think of a tactical team as different pieces in a chess game. The Knight, Rook, Pawn, Bishop, and King each have different moves. The long rifle is comparable to the Queen, the only piece that can move horizontally and diagonally across the board.

RIFLE DATA SHEET			
RIFLE No. DATE			AMMUNITION
	ELEVATION	WINDAGE	REMARKS
100 Yards Position _____			
_____ Yards Position _____			
_____ Yards Position _____			
_____ Yards Position _____			
_____ Yards Position _____			
_____ Yards Position _____			

TOTAL ROUNDS FIRED - RECORD				
Date	Number Of Rounds Fired	Cumulative Total Of Rounds Fired	Name	Remarks

YARD _____ TARGET _____

RANGE	RIFLE AND SCOPE No.		DATE	ELEVATION		WINDAGE	
				Used	Correct	Used	Correct

AMMUNITION	LIGHT	MIRAGE	TEMP.	HOUR	HOLD

LIGHT   WIND

Velocity   Direction

SHOT	1	2	3	4	5	6	7	8	9	10	REMARKS
ELEV											
WIND											
C A L L											

TARGET   DIAGRAM

YARD _____ TARGET _____

RANGE	RIFLE AND SCOPE No.		DATE	ELEVATION		WINDAGE	
				Used	Correct	Used	Correct

AMMUNITION	LIGHT	MIRAGE	TEMP.	HOUR	HOLD

LIGHT   WIND

Velocity   Direction

SHOT	1	2	3	4	5	6	7	8	9	10	REMARKS
ELEV											
WIND											
C A L L											

TARGET   DIAGRAM

RANGE CARD

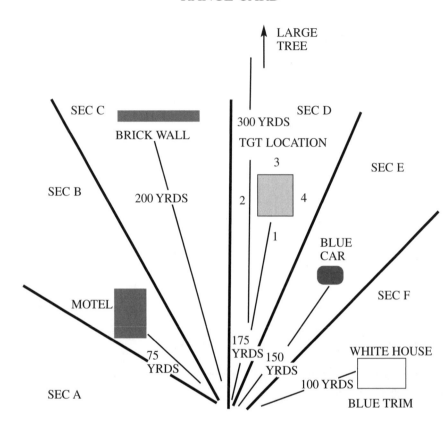

CHAPTER 24

VIP Security

Tactical teams are often called upon to provide security assignments for dignitaries, witnesses, and fellow officers who have been threatened. Although the majority of these assignments are to protect lives, there are increasing incidents of "stalkers" and demonstrators. Recent attacks have included a wide range of targets and methods, all of which must be considered as a possible threat when planning VIP Security. Examples of recent attacks are:

Bomb Attacks

Numerous family planning clinics in the United States

U.S. Marine Barracks - Beirut, Lebanon

Prime Minister - England

World Trade Center - New York

Federal Building - Oklahoma City, Oklahoma

1996 World Olympics - Atlanta, Georgia

Suicide Bomb - Gaza

Suicide Bomb - Jerusalem

U.S. Military Building - Saudi Arabia

U.S. Embassy - Lima, Peru

Pan Am 103 - Scotland

U.S. Embassy - Nairobi, Kenya

U.S. Embassy - Dar es Salaam, Tanzania

Highjacking

TWA Airlines - 1984 Athens, Greece

Cruise Ship "Achille Lauro" 1985 between Italy and Egypt

Tupac Amaru Seizure of Japanese Embassy -Lima, Peru

Members of terrorist group "Al Quaeda" highjacked four U.S. airliners, crashed two into the World Trade Center in New York, one into the Pentagon, and one crashed in Pennsylvania when the passengers attempted to thwart the attack. Approximately 4,000 people were killed. (2001)

Rocket Attack

NATO Commander - Brussels, Belgium

U.S. Embassy - Moscow

U.S. Embassy - Bogota, Colombia

Kidnaping

U.S. Army General - Italy

U.S. Correspondents - Beirut, Lebanon

Embassy Officers - Beirut, Lebanon

DEA Special Agent - Beirut, Lebanon

U.S. Businessmen - Mexico, Colombia, Nicaragua

Kidnaping/Murder

U.S. Ambassador - Kabul, Afghanistan *Kidnappers posed as policemen

U.S. Charge D'AFFAIRES and Embassy Officer - Beirut, Lebanon * Co-opted Embassy Driver

CIA Station Chief - Beirut, Lebanon

U.S. Marine Colonel assigned to U.S. Peacekeeping Force - Beirut, Lebanon

U.S. Ambassador - Khartoum, Sudan

DEA Special Agent - Guadalajara, Mexico

Assassination

U.S. Military Attache - Paris, France

CIA Station Chief - Athens, Greece

President Anwar Sadat - Cairo, Egypt *Islamic Fundamentalists - Military Accomplices

President Indira Ghandi- India *Killed by personal body guard

Prime Minister Shimon Perez - Israel

Two American Diplomats - Karachi, Pakistan

*Attempted assassination U.S. Ambassador's vehicle convoy - Burundi, Africa

In the United States most assassinations, and attempted assassinations have been committed by lone gunmen:

President John F. Kennedy - Rifle

Dr. Martin Luther King - Rifle

Bobby Kennedy - Handgun

Gov. George Wallace - Handgun

President Gerald Ford - Handgun

President Ronald Reagan - Handgun

John Lennon - Handgun

Psychologists have identified attacks on famous people by assailants with low self-esteem and a drive to be recognized as "megacide". They feel that they become as important as the victim elevating their status and the status of their cause. These individuals present a formidable security threat and are predicted to be around for many more years as long as there are groups and individuals who consider themselves disenfranchised and seek attention.

Terrorists generally classify potential targets in terms of accessibility, vulnerability, and political worth (symbolic value). Factors they consider are:

- Risk versus success

- Victim softness versus hardness

- Ease of attack versus value of victim

Soft targets have been accessible to attack, predictable in behavior and daily routine, and unaware of security procedures. Conversely, a hard target has been found to restrict his movements and predictability, exercise security precautions, and demonstrates awareness of surroundings and alertness to danger.

The location of the principal's home and quality of construction is a factor in residential security. Attention should be paid to:

Masonry and woodwork for strength and maintenance

Doors and windows, frames, and bars

Entries and exits for emergency escape and for monitoring visitors

Electronic security system

Traffic flow

Local police

Garbage, mail, lawn care, newspaper routine

Establish a primary and secondary escape and evasion (E and E) route

Domestic employee screening and background check

Install intrusion delay hardware (grills, screens, and deadbolts)

Close window coverings at dusk to prevent monitoring family activities

Fences, walls, dense hedges prevent intrusion; however, shrubbery and decorative fences too near the house can conceal an intruder and should be trimmed or removed

Security teams should be aware of procedures to protect against bomb attacks. This includes awareness of suspicious packages in the mail. Letter and package bomb indicators are:

Protruding wires

Oily stains on wrapping

Lopsided package

Wrong title with name

Strange odor

No return address

Restrictive marking (IE: "personal", "eyes only")

Excessive postage

Mailed from foreign country

Addressed to title only

Rigid or bulky

Badly typed or written

Locations for bomb searches are:

OUTSIDE BUILDING

Trash cans

Dumpsters

Mail boxes

Street drain systems

Storage areas

Parked cars and trucks

INSIDE BUILDING

Mail, parcels, or letters

Restrooms

Trash receptacle

Inside desks

Ceiling with removable panels

Utility closets

Areas hidden by drapes and curtains

Boiler rooms

Under stairwells

Recent repair, patching segments of walls, floors, or ceilings

When traveling, choose high quality hotels as close as possible to where business is conducted. Request another room assignment if one has been reserved in the principal's name. Avoid street level rooms. Determine if the hotel has security guards. Move quickly through entries, exits, and lobbies. Watch for loiterers, unattended luggage, and packages.

There are a number of simple safeguards to protect a principal at his place of business:

Stand away from windows

Place desk away from window

Avoid patterns

Avoid routine trips to office after hours

Be alert to anyone loitering

Use different routes to enter and leave office

Lock restrooms and utility closets

Know location of emergency exits, fire alarms, and fire extin guishers

The initial step for vehicle security is to inspect the car for bombs. Look for telltale signs of tampering such as: pieces of tape or wire, scuff marks or smudges, foreign objects on or near the vehicle, and objects in the tailpipe. The following areas should be visually inspected:

Grill and bumper

Trim and wheel wells - Look for trip wires, ground pressure, or pressure release firing devices

Inspect undercarriage and coil springs

Trunk and rear bumper

Exhaust pipe

Gas tank and cap

Driver and passenger seats

Head rests

Rear seats

Dashboard

Glove compartment

Sun visor

Alarm

Engine compartment

Drive to avoid attack. Vary times and routes. Use different vehicles. Use lead cars and follow cars manned with counter assault teams. Drive close to the center lane to reduce the chance of being forced off the road. Have "safe havens" identified. Know routes to the police and hospitals. Be aware of the areas to avoid.

Drivers should be trained in defensive driving and be able to ram a vehicle to affect an escape. This is accomplished by striking the attacking vehicle in such a way as to force it out of the way. For example, an attacking vehicle pulls in front of the principal vehicle at an angle in an effort to cut it off and force it to stop. By slowing and then accelerating rapidly and striking the attacking vehicle in the rear at an angle, the attacking vehicle will be rammed forward and out of the path of the escaping principal vehicle. If the attacking vehicle stops perpendicular to the principal vehicle, ramming the attacker towards the rear causing that vehicle's engine to act as a fulcrum will spin it out of the way.

Rapidly accelerating in reverse, sharply applying the brakes, and spinning into the other direction is called a "J Turn". Sharply

VIP PROTECTION

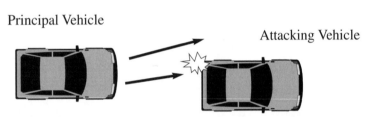

Principal Vehicle

Attacking Vehicle

Principal accelerates and strikes attacker with right front to attacker's left rear and affects escape forward

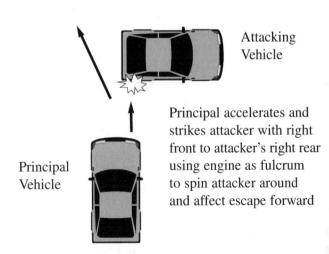

Attacking Vehicle

Principal accelerates and strikes attacker with right front to attacker's right rear using engine as fulcrum to spin attacker around and affect escape forward

Principal Vehicle

applying the parking brake while moving forward, locking the rear wheels, spinning the other direction, unlocking the brake, and accelerating in the other direction is called a "bootleg turn". These tactics should be practiced to where they are done to avoid instinctively stopping to avoid a collision - "chauffeur syndrome".

The security team should train firing from moving vehicles and understand the effects of glass on bullets. Immediate action drills for taking evasive action and putting suppressive fire on attackers should be practiced live fire.

The principles are the same as immediate action drills in an ambush. Study maps and aerial photography of the area to identify likely ambush sites. The key is to escape the ambush site through decisive defensive action. This would often include suppressive fire, and flanking the attacker(s) with a counter assault team. Smoke has been found to be effective to interfere with the attacker's accuracy and mask escape. Grenade launchers, M-203s, and LAWs have been effective counter-ambush weapons. In the Vietnam War, the Viet Cong and North Vietnamese Army used rocket propelled grenades (RPGs) to counter ambushes.

The use of indigenous personnel in protective details has proven to have mixed results. Local police and military officials are knowledgeable of the language, culture, terrain, and often have better intelligence; however, there is a potential for compromise or a failure to react properly under attack. Screening is, of course, recommended for all indigenous personnel. There is an increased practice of using American Military or Department of State Diplomatic Security Service (DSS) personnel exclusively in high-risk foreign countries.

Long rifles should be considered for security assignments. A counter-sniper capability should be included in the vehicle convoy. Sniper/observer teams can also be deployed along the route and at public events attended by the VIP.

For example: If snipers had been deployed along the motorcade route for President Kennedy in Dallas, Texas, there is a high probability that Lee Harvey Oswald would have been observed at the open window in the book depository from where he fired the fatal shots at the President.

If snipers had been deployed to cover the VIP section occupied by Egyptian President Sadat, they would have observed a military truck stop in front of the review stand, soldiers exit and open fire running towards the President's location.

The decision to deploy sniper/observer teams could affect the success of the security assignment, and maybe even world history.

It is recommended to assign no less than four people to the inner perimeter on the principal. One person should be at the immediate left, one to the right front, and two to the rear. This "box" provides 360 degree protection. When the principle moves, the box moves. Never leave the principal. If there is some type of jurisdictional or coordination problem, leave immediately with the principal. When President Sadat entered the grandstand to observe a military parade, military security would not allow his bodyguards to go with him. When the army truck stopped and the assassins exited the truck and rushed the grandstand firing AK-47s, there was no protection for President Sadat. He knew what had occurred, stood up, and faced them. On the other hand, in an assassination attempt on King Hussein of Jordan, his body guards literally piled on top of him. Some were killed, but King Hussein survived.

Information and instruction on bombs are available from BATF. Information on domestic terrorist activity is available from the FBI. Information on assaults and terrorist activity abroad is available from DSS. Training can be arranged from the above agencies, the Secret Service, and military units as well.

CHAPTER 25

Tactical Leadership

Chapter 2 briefly cites some of the basic requirements for a unit commander. Successful SWAT commanders are physically fit and meet all the standards of their unit. They know tactics, weapons, and the strengths and weaknesses of each member of the team. This is best accomplished by qualifying with weapons and ordinance with the team, and training with them to include sharing discomfort and performing the mundane tasks such as picking up brass, stapling targets, setting up the shooting house, and cleaning weapons. The commander should not compete with his men. It is not important that he excel in every phase of training, but that he participate. This will lead to mutual trust and confidence. One of the most critical attributes of a good commander is to function in a crisis effectively and consistently. A good commander listens to his subordinates and employs an open organizational structure with good communication. He must realize he is in command but not in control. Delegation to the assault team leader and sniper/observer teams and trust in their judgement is imperative. A good commander nurtures in training, and leads in battle. It is imperative that the team be confident that the commander makes intelligent decisions consistently under pressure. The commander's superiors must have that same confidence or second guessing, overzealous oversight, and lack of budgetary support will occur.

Management disapproval and lack of support can be displayed in budget cuts or refusal to authorize training or the purchase of weapons and equipment. There is a bias in both the military and civilian police agencies toward elite units and it usually manifests itself in lack of support.

Management of civilian police agencies is extremely concerned with civil liability issues. It would be unfair and unrealistic not address this issue. Lawsuits are increasing for: excessive force, false arrest, negligent training/supervision, and civil rights violations. Large law enforcement agencies pay millions of dollars in awards and settlements each year. Specialized units are held at an even higher standard.

Liability concerns should not impact on decision making when the priority is the protection of life and enforcing the law. Personnel are expected to know and understand the mission, accountability, skills required, the law, and department policy and procedure.

Most common vulnerabilities have been identified as:

- Training

- Experience

- Tactics

- Use of Force

- Compliance with law and policy

- Operational Planning

- Supervision

Training begins with personnel selection. Criteria should include intelligence, confidence, resourcefulness, creativity, flexibility, emotional stability, maturity, physical fitness, and the ability to function well under stress. The operator should be goal oriented and a team player. Evaluations should be written and validated by performance standards. Procedures should be written. Training should be memorialized in individual training files. After action reports, training files, and performance evaluations are subject to discovery in litigation. Training files should also record schools, seminars, leadership training, and professional conferences attended.

Negligent supervision is usually the result of failure to direct and control personnel. Emotional contagion develops among police officers when an officer is assaulted and especially when one is shot. A supervisor may not be able to prevent a bad situation, but may be able to prevent it from becoming worse.

The common sense approach to deciding proper tactics is "reasonableness". Methods should minimize risk of injury and should be taken into consideration when deploying chemical agents and NFDs. Use of negotiators, K-9s, snipers, explosive breaching, and dynamic or non-dynamic entry are critical elements in tactical decision making. Another factor is "necessity." Tactics utilized must not only be reasonable under the circumstances, but must be determined to be necessary to prevent injury or the situation becoming worse.

The minimal use of force must be used to affect the action. This is particularly pertinent to the use of deadly force. Deadly force must be related to a direct threat. Fire control and discipline are essential.

All team members, and especially the commander, must know the law. The Fourth Amendment, search and seizure, knock and notice, and other criminal statutes must be adhered to.

Additionally, the commander must know policy in regards to high-risk events, barricaded suspects, criteria to activate SWAT, use of NFDs, chemical agents, explosive ordinance, less lethal munitions, rescue vehicles, and other specialized logistics. The commander must know specific notification procedures to include review and approval.

Operational plans must be standardized and in written form. These plans will be closely scrutinized. Photographs and video of the target site are recommended. Supervisory review of plans must be documented.

The commander must know acceptable tactics and policy. He must enforce policy, review all plans, supervise mission execution, control team actions, and be available for decision making. Many events can be projected and procedures coordinated in advance. For example, an officer involved shooting checklist could be prepared and coordinated with the prosecuting attorney's office and chain of command. Basically it should include:

- Advise chain of command

- Secure scene

- Request ambulance

- Establish perimeter security

- Identify officer who discharged firearm

- Request additional personnel if necessary

- Notify local precinct/station

- Locate and identify witnesses

- Walk through scene with officer

- Record date, time, location, assignment, officers involved, witnesses, firearms (make, model, serial number), rounds fired, suspects, injured parties, property damage, vehicles, and evidence. Diagrams with photographs should record position of officers and suspects, witnesses, vehicles, buildings, path of bullet, ejected shell casings, and any other pertinent evidence.

Civilian law enforcement agencies have become like corporate America with an emphasis on civil liability placing a price tag term of reference to enforcing the law. There is an emphasis on EEO, sexual harassment, community policing, and blood born pathogens training and less budgeting for not only tactical training and equipment but firearms qualification as well. During "DESERT STORM", JCS Commander General Colin Powell never asked what the cost of winning the war would be. He concentrated on winning and let others concentrate on paying for it later.

Law enforcement agencies have developed a bunker mentality where they perceive danger from everything outside their inner circle of managers, most whose sole purpose in life is the survival of the agency and to maintain, or enhance their status in that agency. This predictably causes management to stampede away from every issue that is a perceived threat. The most common mechanism is called "Tombstone Management". After an officer is killed, the department conducts and investigation to determine culpability and adjusts policy to "lessons learned". Another management technique is the "Kaopectate Syndrome". If one officer gets diarrhea, every officer must take Kaopectate. This superficial exercise absolves management of any responsibility, in their eyes. After all, if an officer is killed by a criminal, the criminal is to blame.

The use of SWAT Teams, K-9, and snipers can cause negative publicity and public reaction in some circles. By not deploying them, this negative reaction is averted, and if an officer is killed, the criminal is prosecuted, and the department most often gets positive news coverage for the officer's funeral. Departments set up memorial funds, sponsor memorial golf tournaments, and invite the slain officer's family to their Christmas parties. In their eyes they are totally absolved.

The current lack of strong leadership in law enforcement is not an unexpected phenomenon. Law enforcement expanded and increased in professionalism in the 1960s. College educated, goal oriented, hands on managers who were respected for "risk taking" rose up in their agencies to command positions. The most successful SWAT Team Commanders and commanders of special operations units in the military had a trait of lethality, often called "the eye of the tiger". They also had a tendency to display an "icy calm" when commanding combat situations. They were "man-hunters" that relied on their instincts. Thirty years later, they are retiring

Law enforcement has changed management styles with an emphasis on self-inspection, liability prevention, and less aggressive conflict resolution methods. Risk taking is discouraged. Pandemonium in the command post and bad decisions are more common place. This has resulted in a decrease in productivity, lack of mission orientation, and decreased morale. Law enforcement will have to retool itself, as the military did, to meet the demands of the next millennium.

When I was in the DEA, we called the military the "Big Dog". When ever we needed logistics or training, we would turn to the military. Another example of their support is the invasion of Panama, "Operation Just Cause", in December 1989 when they apprehended Panamanian President Manuel Noriega on a DEA indictment. They sustained 31 killed in action during that operation. They accomplished their mission. DEA has a saying: "You can't run with the big dogs, if you pee like a puppy." I will never forget the support I received from my brothers and sisters in the military. They are the embodiment of the term "American".

CHAPTER 26

Tactical Operations Center

The Tactical Operations Center (TOC) concept was developed to support the overall tactical mission by providing crisis site intelligence to the tactical commander for use against the adversary. Essential Elements of Information (EEI) are collected from witnesses, investigative follow-up, released hostages, sniper observation, crisis negotiations, technical surveillance, aerial photography, public records, floor plans, scouting, and movement patterns of the adversary, and reported to the tactical commander.

The TOC is not a command and control unit. It does not replace the Command Post. It is an ad hoc support function to provide EEI to the tactical commander. It is usually commanded by an officer of equal rank to the tactical commander with the authority to "get things done". Staffing requires specially trained personnel with a background in tactics and, preferably, intelligence analysis. It has been found that it is best not to have a large staff. Recommended staffing would include:

1. TOC Coordinator

2. Assistant Coordinator

3. Intelligence/Investigative Member

4. Sniper Control (Two Person Minimum)

5. Field Command Liaison if Necessary

The TOC can be set up in a building away from the public and the media. It should be large enough to accommodate the staff, display EEI on the walls, and conduct briefings for the assault team, snipers, and negotiators. An area nearby for the assault team to practice entry is preferable. It is also preferable to have a helicopter landing zone (HLZ) nearby.

The following EEI should be displayed on the walls:

1. Location/Target

2. Terrorists/ hostage taker

3. Hostages

4. Weapons

5. Explosives

6. Demands/Deadlines

7. Witnesses

8. Medical problems

9. Floor plans

10. Target photos

11. Vehicles

12. Maps

13. Utilities

14. Surrounding area

15. Light/Weather data

The above categories should be pre-printed, although they can be made out in long hand if necessary and adapted to the situation.

One of the benefits of the TOC is that it can set up with a minimum of effort in a short period of time. The entire TOC kit can be contained in two briefcases and stored in the logistics vehicle for the team. The following are suggested items to be stored in the kit:

- 2 - briefcases
- 4 - pieces of 30 X 30 clear plastic
- 1 - flash light
- 1 - Polaroid camera with six packs of film
- 4 - boxes map tacks: blue, red, white, green
- 8 - legal tablets
- pencils, pens, erasers, paper clips, staplers
- 2 - rolls duct tape
- 2 - rolls masking tape
- various colors markers and pens
- 4 - rulers
- paper
- field interview cards
- emergency procedures check list
- 2 - "Janes Pocket Book on Pistols and Submachine Guns"
- Pre-printed debriefing check list
- TOC handbook
- 1 - cellular telephone

Initial EEI requirements for tactical deployment and emergency assault are as follows:

1. HOSTAGES
   a. Total number
   b. Male/Female
   c. Ages
   d. Clothing description
   e. Location within target site
   f. How detained - Where guarded

2. TERRORISTS /HOSTAGE TAKERS
   a. Total number (Leader if Known)
   b. Weapons - amount and type
   c. Explosives - Booby Traps - Where
   d. Protective vests - Masks
   e. General description if available

3. TARGET SITE
   a. Quick description and floor plan
   b. Location of Terrorists
   c. Location of Hostages
   d. Barricaded Doors or Windows
   e. Dogs or Pets Inside
   f. Anti-intrusion devices
   g. Location and number of telephones and numbers

The following format is for hostage/witness debriefing:

1. WITNESS/HOSTAGE/ OTHER SOURCE NAME

2. HOSTAGE INFORMATION
   a. Total number
   b. Age/Sex/Race

c. Significant medical health problems

d. Distinguishing physical features (tatoos, limp, eye glasses, height, weight, hair and eye color)

e. Language spoken and degree of proficiency

f. Clothing (colors, sizes, style, hats)

g. Locations - utilize floor plans

>   Day
>
>   Night
>
>   Eating Periods
>
>   Exercise Periods

h. Sympathy to terrorists

i. How detained/secured and How guarded

j. Other

3. TERRORISTS

a. Total number

b. Patterns developed

>   Movement and location of guards
>
>   >   Day
>   >
>   >   Night
>
>   Eating habits
>
>   Attitude
>
>   Reactions to negotiations
>
>   Reactions to food deliveries
>
>   Unusual reactions to selected hostages

c. What established organizations are represented by terrorists

d. Location of Terrorist CP

e. Probable terrorist reaction to armed assault

f. Amount of food

g. Amount of sleep

h. Use of drugs/alcohol

i. Any contact with outside individuals

j. Use of intrusion/Early warning devices

k. Weapons

> Type and Quantity
>
> Ammunition

l. Explosives

> Type of device
>
> Firing system
>
> Amount of explosive
>
> Booby trap
>
> Remote control
>
> Placement
>
> Condition of device

m. Following data on each terrorist

> Name or number if utilized
>
> Weapons
>
> Explosives
>
> Location (Day, Night, Guard Duty)
>
> Role
>
> Attitude
>
> Apparent training

Degree of dedication

Use of telephones and communication (How many and where)

Special equipment (binoculars, night vision devices, protective mask, body armor etc.)

Clothing

Who maintains telephone contact

Length of cords to telephones

Telephone numbers

4. BARRICADE AREA, BUILDING, PLANE, CONVEYANCE

   a. Schematic drawing of target

      Include all dimensions of rooms, hallways, doorways, windows, and other openings between floors, exterior/interior of building, plane, or conveyance

   b. Schematic drawing of compound and surrounding area

   c. Entry points

      • Doors (type, thickness, locks, hinges, barricaded, booby traps, opening functions)

      • Windows (type, thickness, locked/unlocked, barricaded, booby trapped, describe opening functions)

      • Special accesses to elevators, stairwells, light shafts, and air conditioning ducts

The dynamics of the TOC provide the tactical commander with up to the minute EEI. It is logged and posted as it is received to establish patterns and vulnerabilities. One of the most useful factors is that it prevents information from being overlooked, forgotten, or not being analyzed in the proper context. For example, it might be learned that a hostage is law enforcement or military, or has a background in one or both disciplines. Then the determination must be made as to what action that hostage might take during an assault. Particular attention would be paid to positively identify and locate that hostage. Another critical factor would be patterns of movement that would lead to an open air assault to end the crisis. On the other hand, the more EEI developed on the terrorists/hostage taker, the more the negotiators have to work with to resolve the crisis without assaulting and risking lives.

CHAPTER 27

Hostage Negotiations and Rescue

Negotiations should be initiated with the hostage taker at the earliest. Although communications are usually by telephone, P.A. systems, and specialized telephones designed to be used in negotiations can be utilized. Experience has shown that it is not beneficial to prolong negotiations after an initial period of time has passed to stabilize the situation and "buy time" for the snipers to deploy and for the assault team to rehearse entry. Most violence on hostages occurs within the first 45 minutes. The negotiator must be aware that the use of deadly force is highly probable and not feel that negotiations are unsuccessful if the hostage taker is neutralized.

It is imperative that negotiators train in life-like scenarios with the tactical team. The command level of the department should be briefed on all procedures. The tactical commander should have as close a relationship with the negotiations team and understand their function as with the assault team members.

Negotiators and command personnel must realize that threats made by the hostage taker must be taken as genuine in view of the life threatening ramifications not only to the hostage, but innocent bystanders and law enforcement personnel. Command personnel are encouraged to make the decision to use deadly force based on the following suggested criteria:

1. Does the terrorist/hostage taker have a hostage?

2. Has a threat to kill a hostage been made?

3. Can it be verified?

If the answer is "yes", then deadly force is the necessary option.

The tactical commander must realize that an opportunity to successfully resolve the situation might be brief. He must be able to make a decision quickly to exploit the vulnerability.

The most effective option is the sniper or "open air assault". This is due to the high probability of success. Two highly skilled marksmen using sophisticated, accurate equipment are required for each suspect target. The most effective deployment is the "L" shaped configuration.

Target identification is critical. Coordination with the TOC Sniper Control is essential. All shots must be simultaneous on command by the Sniper Controller. Head shots are the most effective. The ground assault team must be deployed in conjunction with the marksmen to follow up immediately.

In the event the situation goes mobile, the "open air" option is still the most effective, because of the exposure of the suspects. Vehicle or linear assaults can be initiated by marksmen depending on the conveyance. This contingency should be planned for early on in the situation.

The dynamic assault hostage rescue is the least desirable option. It requires precision teamwork, large numbers of personnel, multi-channel communications, and close quarter battle with the potential for multiple shots.

The following are outlines for suggested procedures for resolving barricaded suspect/hostage situations:

1. Contact hostage negotiating team

2. Establish inner perimeter

3. Establish outer perimeter

4. Designate arrest team

5. Restrict radio frequency

6. Request helicopter and Identify landing zone

7. Establish Command Post and TOC

8. Determine if a crime has been committed and locate victims.

9. Obtain telephone number of location

10. Maintain chronological log of events

11. Contact suspects by telephone or PA

12. Evacuate surrounding buildings

13. Contact emergency services (ambulance, fire, paramedic, red cross)

14. Select location to brief press

15. Obtain floor plan of target location

16. Obtain essential elements of information regarding suspects

17. Identify individuals that have influence with the suspect/s

18. Have handling crew remain available at command post to meet with SWAT Team Leader or his designate

19. Do not allow suspects to leave location

20. Do not allow individuals (friends, relatives) to enter location

21. As field personnel are relieved by SWAT, have them report to CP for additional assignments

22. Crowd control after situation is resolved

23. Handling unit obtain report from SWAT Team Leader or designate

24. Clean up CP - express appreciation to neighbors and assisting civilians

25. When possible, critique the operation with those involved

CHAPTER 28

Physical and Psychological Trauma

Law enforcement and military personnel are faced with psychologically, physically stressful, and traumatic situations on a routine basis; especially, but not limited to, shooting incidents. The total number of in the line of duty deaths of police officers is declining, but the number of deaths as a result of gunfire is increasing. In 1994, more police officers died of suicide than were killed in the line of duty. In fact twice as many. Work related stress is undoubtedly a major factor. Commanders should know how to recognize stress indicators in themselves and others, and appropriate coping mechanisms.

There are a number of physiological reactions that occur when a stressful incident occurs. The cerebral cortex greatly decreases activity affecting recollection, analytical capability, auditory ability (sound is suppressed), and vision. Action appears to be in slow motion. Tunnel vision/binocular vision occurs and greatly affects a sight picture thus reducing accuracy. The hypothalamus stimulates the adrenal gland. Adrenal corticotropin Hormone (ACTH) is a hormone secreted by the adrenal gland in combat. This causes an increased heart rate, pupils dilate, the digestive process stops, capillaries constrict, blood rushes to the skeletal muscles, breathing becomes rapid and shallow. Sensitivity to pain diminishes. Acid is triggered in the stomach and sometimes after repetitive periods, causes bleeding. The sensations are often described as heart pounding, breathlessness, and an empty feeling or sick feeling in the stomach. Prolonged and repetitive secretions of adrenaline can even cause a scarring of the heart called Mycosis.

These physiological reactions are sometimes interpreted as fear, "having your heart in your mouth." Training and immediate action drills help overcome the emotional reaction to the physical stimuli. Courage is a quality of mind that helps people face danger or hardship. Courage is a quality of a warrior that enables him to do the hard things. "Who will do the hard things? He who can."

Noradrenaline is a chemical that results from post stress syndrome. It suppresses memory and causes sensory distortion. This is one of the reasons why "eye witness" accounts vary so greatly. Many times anterograde amnesia occurs where the subject forgets what occurred just prior to the stressful incident. Many subjects experience perseveration which is repeated thought of the incident. Other post trauma stress reactions are:

- Fatigue
- Anxiety and tension
- Sadness, crying, and depression
- Hyper alertness
- Guilt feeling about incident
- Trouble concentrating
- Anger

- Excessive drinking
- Infidelity
- Headaches
- Backaches
- Muscle spasms
- Teeth clenching during sleep
- Insomnia
- Bad dreams
- Impotence
- Withdrawal from loved ones
- Irritability
- Becoming argumentative
- Excessive aggression
- Passiveness ("hiding")
- Poor memory
- Poor judgement
- Loss of appetite
- Angry outbursts
- Mood swings
- Poor personal hygiene, physical appearance and grooming

There is also potential secondary trauma that is caused by how the operator is treated after the incident. The post incident investigation, joking, congratulations, repeated questioning, and even friendly physical contact can cause further stress. Many times co-workers do not know what to do or say and their lack of contact is interpreted by the operator as disapproval or abandonment ("freezing").

Some of the suggested ways of coping with stress are:

Share the experience with others who are close. The family especially, they know something is wrong.

Sense of humor

Return to normal routine as soon as possible

Maintain a physical fitness schedule

Religion

Keep mind off incident

Learn a relaxation exercise that will relax the body and clear the mind. Be alert to an emotional reaction to objects and scenes that remind you of the incident (weapons, uniform, office, scene of incident, other). Visualize these objects and practice relaxing exercises until they no longer cause anxiety.

Another coping technique is to list hobbies or recreational activities you enjoyed as a child. Select one activity and do it within one week. Next make a list of hobbies or recreational activities that you have always wanted to do. Make plans to do one of these activities within two weeks.

Although clinicians, friends, and family are all-important factors in dealing with post incident trauma, the first step and most important act in the coping process is in the individual himself. Everyone should be alert to the effects of stress and how to cope with it before it affects an individual's health, effectiveness, and he becomes a liability to the team and mission.

CHAPTER 29

Future of SWAT and Special Military Units

On December 17, 1997, Peruvian rebels (Tupac Amaru) stormed the Japanese Embassy in Lima, Peru and held 72 hostages demanding the release of imprisoned comrades. The rebels threatened to kill hostages if their demands were not met. Negotiations came to an impasse on March 12. On April 22, after a 126-day standoff, 140 Peruvian soldiers assaulted the embassy from tunnels dug under the embassy, and the roof using explosive breaching, and rescued 71 hostages, one hostage was killed, two soldiers were killed, and all 14 rebels were killed. Explosive breaching, and dynamic assault tactics were decisive.

On February 28, 1997, two bank robbers armed with assault rifles were engaged by Los Angeles Police patrol officers. The robbers wore body armor and kept LAPD at bay with suppressing automatic weapons fire. During the attempted escape, one suspect killed himself with a single shot to the head with a handgun. The second suspect attempted to commandeer a vehicle. LAPD SWAT engaged him with automatic weapons. The officers exited their vehicle and initiated suppressive automatic weapons fire from positions of cover. One officer fired at an angle at the pavement and ricocheted rounds into the suspect's legs. The suspect died of multiple gunshot wounds. Special Weapons and Tactics were decisive.

The above two incidents are examples of the current tactical threat. A large number of hostages can be taken anywhere in the world at any time by a number of terrorist or criminal organizations. Hostage situations that occur in a foreign country would be the responsibility of JSOC. Domestic hostage incidents would be either FBI/HRT, or state and local jurisdiction. Furthermore, enforcement is constantly at risk of encountering heavily armed suspects as in the Los Angeles bank robbery.

Incidents of attacks by Islamic fundamentalist terrorist organizations on American tourists and businessmen have increased in the Middle East and Southwest Asia. Kidnaping of American businessmen by criminals in foreign countries has increased. Attacks in the United States by terrorists are also increasing. There are more terrorist groups and criminal elements targeting Americans than ever before. The threat of attack by well armed, trained, and organized groups is a clear and present danger.

On September 11, 2001, nineteen members of the terrorist group, "Al Quaeda" (the Base) headed by Saudi Arabian exile Osama Bin Laden, highjacked four airliners:

American Airlines Flight # 11 (Boeing 767) from Boston scheduled for Los Angeles – total onboard – 92

United Airlines Flight # 175 (Boeing 767) from Boston scheduled for Los Angeles– total onboard - 65

These two aircraft were crashed into the World Trade Center twin towers in New York City.

American Airlines Flight #77 (Boeing 757) from Dulles (Washington D. C.) scheduled for Los Angeles – total onboard 64 – crashed into the Pentagon in Virginia near Washington, D. C.

<u>United Airlines Flight #93</u> (Boeing 757) – total onboard 45 – scheduled from Newark, New Jersey for San Francisco crashed in Pennsylvania when passengers attempted to thwart the attack. It is suspected that the intended target was the Capitol building.

Approximately 4,000 people were killed representing 80 countries including the 266 passengers onboard the airliners. This has been identified, by many, as the worst intelligence failure in the history of the United States. The United States government has been restructured to prevent further breakdowns and failures in the intelligence and federal law enforcement community.

There is a saying: "If it's predictable. It's preventable." It can certainly be predicted that there will be deadly, large scale, engagements in the future. What can be prevented are law enforcement or military unit casualties. Casualties can be prevented by tactical training and specialized equipment to meet the threat.

AP/Wide World Photos

Until September 11, 2001, it was not politically correct to support an expansion of counter-terrorist capability and SWAT equipment and training for law enforcement. Recent congressional hearings relative to incidents of a tactical nature in the United States that have caused negative publicity have indicated a sensitivity to the "militarization" of domestic law enforcement. As a result, law enforcement agencies are "softening" their terminology. Snipers are "forward observers" or "scouts". When they shoot, it is an "open air assault". Diversionary devices are called "noise flash devices". Aimed Quick Kills are "shoulder aimed fire". The assault command for the entry "execute" is changed to "initiate".

The next time a hostage is rescued, it is recommended that he be asked if he was offended that to save his life a sniper killed the hostage taker with a round placed center brain. He should be asked if he was offended by the loud sound and bright flash of an NFD, and if he cared what it is called, or if the assault team was too aggressive in the execution of the rescue, or if their terminology was offensive.

The future of SWAT is destined to entail increased training and further development of equipment. Doctrine will be established and a national standard will be accepted as the norm. This will be a result not only of an increase in the professionalism of law enforcement in general, but as a result of negative case law in litigation. Law enforcement would be remiss in not taking advantage of the expertise and hundreds of millions of dollars spent in the research and development of special operations equipment the Department of Defense has spent in the tactical and counter terrorist arena such as weapons that neutralize enemy electronic equipment.

There are a number of initiatives the U. S. Government can take to meet the foreign security threat. Embassy Marine Guards can be equipped and trained for a limited immediate action hostage rescue. It is unrealistic to expect JSOC to respond to a 'FLASH' teletype from a foreign country and expect them to deploy from North Carolina when hostage takers are dumping dead hostages out of an embassy window every hour until their demands are met. The expansion of DELTA and pre-deployment of DELTA operators and SEALs to predetermined "flash points" would enhance response time.

State Department DSS could establish Counter Assault Team (CAT) follow cars at high risk locations and increase DSS inner perimeter personnel on protective details for Ambassadors. Experience has shown that terrorists abort when their chance of success is diminished. Furthermore, the larger the security detail, the larger the assault force is required to attack success-fully. The larger the terrorist cell, the better chances of intelli-gence becoming aware of the operation.

A mechanism to pass real time classified intelligence to law enforcement agencies should be developed. The federal govern-ment and intelligence agencies are over protective of their wire tap, HUMINT, SIGINT, and ELINT capability and restrict dis-semination. The large majority of the product is not that sensi-tive and it would not damage national security if sources and methods were divulged in court. Furthermore, there is case law supporting not divulging sensitive sources and methods. SWAT Team Commanders could be given security clearances to act as liaison with government agencies and act as contact points to "wall off" the information. The SWAT Team would take action because their Commander told them to, and does not have a "need to know" the classified information. The government has conducted money laundering and counter-drug operations for years with this type of arrangement with state and local agencies.

Throughout history societies have had classes in their social structure. Almost all societies have had a "warrior class" for protection. Society depends on warriors to do the hard things. There will always be those who want to serve their country, protect, and rescue the innocent, and enforce the law. Different societies refer to them as a "prince," an "avenging angel," the "sword and shield" or "the sons of God." Society will always need warriors.

About the Author

Michael Holm retired from the U.S. Drug Enforcement Administration (DEA) as Assistant Special Agent in Charge in Los Angeles, California, and is credited with making with the world's largest drug seizure in history (21,700 kilograms of cocaine).

His assignments included Chief of Europe, Middle East Desk in DEA Headquarters, Group Supervisor Chicago, Illinois; SWAT Team Commander Detroit, Michigan; Country Attache Cairo, Egypt; and he was also assigned to Beirut, Lebanon; Kabul, Afghanistan; Del Rio, Texas; Miami, Florida; and Seattle, Washington.

He earned a Bachelor of Science in Police Science and Administration at Washington State University before becoming a Police Officer with the Seattle Police Department in 1968. He joined DEA in 1969 and served extensively on special assignments worldwide throughout his career. Mike is currently the owner and operator of a resort and recently graduated from Northern Michigan University with a Masters of Public Administration with areas of concentration in Criminal Justice and American Foreign Policy. He is a Criminal Justice Professor, lectures on government law enforcement operations, a tactical instructor for law enforcement agencies and an international consultant.

INDEX

ORDER FORM

Toll Free: 800-732-3659
Telephone: 913-385-2034
Fax: 913-385-2039
Online: www.varropress.com
Postal: Varro Press, Inc.
             P.O. Box 8413
             Shawnee Mission, Kansas USA 66208

Have your credit card information ready.

Swat Team Development and Deployment

Qty. _____ @ $29.95 each $ _____

Shipping: *
First book $5.00 $ _____
Additional copies $1.00 each $ _____

TOTAL $ _____

* Priority shipping or foreign: *Call 913-385-2034 or visit us online at varropress.com*

Ordered By:
Name: _____
Address: _____
City: _____ State _____ ZIP: _____
Country: _____
Telephone: _____

Ship To: *(If different from above.)*
Name: _____
Address: _____
City: _____ State _____ ZIP: _____
Country: _____
Telephone: _____

Payment:
☐ Check
☐ Credit Card
     ☐ VISA   ☐ MasterCard   ☐ AMEX   ☐ Discover
Card Number: _____ Exp. Date: _____
Name on Card: _____
Signature: _____

ORDER FORM

Toll Free: 800-732-3659
Telephone: 913-385-2034

Have your credit card information ready.

Fax: 913-385-2039
Online: www.varropress.com
Postal: Varro Press, Inc.
P.O. Box 8413
Shawnee Mission, Kansas USA 66208

Swat Team Development and Deployment

Qty. _____ @ $29.95 each $ _____

Shipping: *
First book $5.00 $ _____
Additional copies $1.00 each $ _____

TOTAL $ _____

* Priority shipping or foreign: *Call 913-385-2034 or visit us online at varropress.com*

Ordered By:
Name: _____
Address: _____
City: _____ State _____ ZIP: _____
Country: _____
Telephone: _____

Ship To: *(If different from above.)*
Name: _____
Address: _____
City: _____ State _____ ZIP: _____
Country: _____
Telephone: _____

Payment:
☐ Check
☐ Credit Card
    ☐ VISA   ☐ MasterCard   ☐ AMEX   ☐ Discover
Card Number: _____ Exp. Date: _____
Name on Card: _____
Signature: _____